WHAT CHRISTIAN LEADI
FATHER TEACH ME H

John A. Shomade's writing lays out the power of God's Love in strong, biblical and practical ways. Men and women will find encouragement to live a love-inspired life as they read the powerful principles and testimonies found in this book.

ELD. JONATHAN M. WYNNE M.A., M.B.A., M.ED.
AUTHOR, BIBLE TEACHER, CONSULTANT

In our world today where many seek love in all the wrong places, the author offers a powerful guidance on trusting God—who is LOVE and the SOURCE of all good things—to help us love others. That's a highly needed message that should be shared everywhere!

C. PASCHAL EZE, AUTHOR AND DIRECTOR OF SPIRITUAL LIFE AND PR AT
THE 1909-FOUNDED DETROIT RESCUE MISSION MINISTRIES, USA

This is one of the holiest prayers which God can never ignore when sincerely uttered. It's only next to asking directly for the will of the Father to be done in one's life always. Therefore I strongly believe this book will be a great blessing and spiritual refreshing to many readers who meditate on its contents in its right context. Rev. John Shomade has written another book worthy of meditation by all seekers of love. It can only be inspired by the Holy Spirit. I gladly endorse and recommend this book, *Father Teach Me How to Love Again.*

APOSTLE THOMAS OJO, CHRIST TEMPLE INTERNATIONAL

The writing style is excellent, the poise is outstanding, the style is dynamic, great grace and poetic symbolism marks this ever needed book in and outside the body of Christ. Divine inspiration and excellent writing style of the author makes one want to pick up the book and sit with it for hours without wanting to put the book down.

I recommend and attest to the fact that God commissioned the author to bring clarification and enlightenment of this mystery in simple terms for us all to know, comprehend and be imparted with the love of God.

JOSES HIZKIAH, UNFAILING LIFE INT'L MINISTRY

FATHER
TEACH ME HOW TO
LOVE AGAIN

JOHN AKEEM SHOMADE

BRIDGE
LOGOS

Newberry, FL 32669

Bridge-Logos
Newberry, FL 32669

Father, Teach Me How to Love Again:
The Love Factor
By John Akeem Shomade

Copyright © 2018 Bridge-Logos

Printed in the United States of America

International Standard Book Number: 978-1-61036-471-3

Library of Congress Catalog Card Number: 2018931857

Cover/Interior design by Kent Jensen | knail.com

Cover photo: Helena Lopes, pexels.com

Unless otherwise indicated, all Scriptures quotations are from the Holy Bible: *New International Version* (NIV). © 1973, 1978, 1984 by International Bible Society. Used by permission of Zondervan Publishing House.

Scripture quotations marked KJV are from the King James Version of the Bible (Public Domain).

Those marked NKJV are from the New King James Version. © 1982 by Thomas Nelson, Inc. Used by permission. All rights reserved.

Scripture quotations marked NASB are taken from the *New American Standard Bible,* © 1960, 1962, 1963, 1968, 1971, 1972, 1973, 1975, 1977 by The Lockman Foundation.

Scripture quotations marked NLT are taken from the Holy Bible, New Living Translation, © 1996, 2004, 2007 by Tyndale House Foundation. Used by permission of Tyndale House Publishers, Inc., Carol Stream, Illinois 60188, USA. All rights reserved.

Scripture quotations marked AMP are taken from the Amplified® Bible, copyright © 2015 by The Lockman Foundation. Used by permission.

Dedication

*To all those living in sacrificial love throughout the world—
please don't give up as God will never forget your labor of love.*

*To the body of Christ for carrying the good news of God's love
to every part of the world—your reward is first on this earth
and then in eternity.*

*To my family, friends, and well-wishers who have shown me
practical demonstration of God's love—thank you for your love,
may His agape love never leave nor forsake you.*

*To my wife and children—you have witnessed love in action
and the transformation that comes after the Father decided
to dwell with us in love. May you always be protected and
motivated by His agape love.*

*We have walked this route of love together, sometimes in joy
and other times with pain in our heart. As we continue to grow
up together in love, I want to reassure all of you that God loves
you and that I love you too with the love of Christ. We all must*

walk together in love, being the second greatest commandment of God.

Thanks for all our years in the past and present, and thanks in advance for the greater years to come if Christ tarries. The banner of God over us is love.

Jesus replied: "'Love the Lord your God with all your heart and with all your soul and with all your mind.' This is the first and greatest commandment. And the second is like it: 'Love your neighbor as yourself.' All the Law and the Prophets hang on these two commandments." (Matthew 22:37-40)

Contents

Foreword

In our world of today, love is probably one of the most misunderstood, misinterpreted, misapplied words across the generations. From the perspective of two young individuals attracted to one another in a sexual relationship with or without any long term firm commitment, they are in love. To the parent or carer who will sacrifice practically anything for their child or ward, they do this because they love.

To complicate matters, there is the love that the unique creator of the world and universe has for mankind that led him to sacrifice himself as the ultimate price of Redemption of mankind. How these various perspectives and perceptions of love fit together as pieces of a jigsaw puzzle to produce a complete picture of love is the core question this book looks to answer.

The scope of love goes beyond the common notions and views we have held for decades. A major aspect of love covered eloquently is forgiveness. Love makes it possible for those who have been hurt emotionally by the vicissitudes of life to heal through the tool of love-based forgiveness. A link between love and discipline from the angle of tough love is explored extensively in this book and some far reaching conclusions are drawn from this discourse.

The author in this brilliant book unpacks the multifaceted dimensions of love in nine practical invigorating chapters. Each chapter provides an in-depth insight into the various flavours, varieties and applications of love to our daily lives. The book draws on many reservoirs of knowledge from a range of authorities to provide a clinical direction of the subject matter. Every reader will gain a comprehensive revelation of the purpose of love with this easy to read book that is brilliant in its simplicity yet robust in its literary detail.

A whole chapter is devoted to providing a clear oversight into the role of erotica love in intimacy among married couples, the writing seeks to debunk many myths on this subject. Tips on rejuvenating relationships and keeping them evergreen are offered in this chapter and it will certainly prove helpful to all.

This is a treasure our world needs to rediscover to provide a real panacea to our confused hurting and often complex world of constant paradoxes. I commend this book to you as a tool and resource to rekindle true love in all areas of our lives. May you learn to truly love again!

—Pastor Stephen Bello
Vice Chairman, Churches Together in Medway, Kent

Preface

And hope does not put us to shame, because God's love has been poured out into our hearts through the Holy Spirit, who has been given to us. (Romans 5:5)

This book was birthed out of my desire to see God's people reactivate, rediscover, and resurrect the power of love in their lives. On a personal note, I wrote this book not because I am perfect in love; on the contrary, I am a student of love, learning to walk on a daily basis in the overflowing love of God shed abroad in my heart by the Holy Spirit. As a son of God, I know beyond reasonable doubt that God loves me unconditionally.

Love is the answer to most of the ailments in the world today because the healing power of love brings emotional healing, and this leads to good relationships with one another and often physical healing. The pressures of the modern world crowd out love in our society and there is an erosion of community spirit and family values. Our love tank is dangerously running on the empty and we cannot give what we do not have. The youths of the nations are left to fend for themselves, while the adults are looking after "self." Compassion and neighborhood cooperation have given way to neighborhood animosity. Disputes are now settled in court rather than by applying the "love thy neighbor" principle.[1]

In fact, a secular group called Rose Royce puts it succinctly in their song "Love Don't Live Here Anymore" (1978). Just as Rose Royce sang about the disappearance of love in our environment, perhaps love has really been abandoned. It would appear this group saw into to the future because, thirty years ago, that song was made famous by the above-named group and we are witnessing the death of love in the world on an unprecedented scale.

Love came to live with us at the time of new birth. He dwelt inside us and we felt invisible. Nothing is impossible for us and trouble seems far away because the greatest Lover dwells with us until we are changed into His image. We drove Him away with our worldly attitudes: hatred, jealousy, backbiting, animosity, bitterness, and the like. So love doesn't live here anymore. What remains of love is just emptiness and memories of what we once had. He's gone to find another place to dwell, a place where He would be appreciated and not considered weak for caring. We must cry in repentance and call Him back, for He is our Life.

I want to encourage every reader of this book that the love of God has not gone away. You are love resurrected because the Beholder of love, who promised never to leave nor forsake you, lives inside you now. In fact, He is with you always, calling you, romancing you, and waiting patiently for you to come back to your "first love." He is knocking at the door of your heart every second, asking for permission to come into your life and to fill your life with a new kind of love that goes beyond emotion, sentiments, romance, and the erotic. God is ready to fill you with

---

1   Luke 10:27, 36-37; Deuteronomy 6:5; Leviticus 19:18.

a love that is birthed from the heart of the Father and He loves all his children enough to send His one and only Son to the world to die for the sin of humankind.

When you open your heart to Him and remain in Him, you will never be found wanting in the love department again because the greatest Lover, one who never will disappoint, never leave nor forsake you, lives inside you. All you have to do is to come into a wholehearted relationship with Him today and develop passion, great affection, and adoration towards Him and watch Him love, romance, and touch you in places newly discovered in your heart. Watch Him shower you with divine affection, passion, and favor previously unknown to you. The name of this Lover is Jesus Christ.

In this book, you will learn how to rediscover the Father's love and walk in it again, irrespective of your age, experience, failure, gender, pain, profession, or religious preference. God loves you passionately, and if you were the only person left on earth, He would have sent His Son to come and save you. He would have died just for you to ensure that you have eternal life starting from planet earth.

This book is simply a sequel to my first book, *The Fear Factor*, and more specifically the chapter "From Fear to Love," where, amongst other things, I looked at the definition of love, compared fear and love, and discussed the temptation to imitate love and the benefits of walking in love. I then finished by encouraging readers to let perfect love cast out fear. The focus of this book is to learn how to release ourselves into the arms of our loving Father like a baby in order to receive and resurrect the power of love in our lives again.

Are you drained and exhausted? Is your love tank leaking or showing red danger signs? Have you tried everything in your power and nothing is working? Has the pressure of our modern living stifled out love of the Father in you? Is your marriage or relationship with the brethren disintegrating and you don't know how to put it back? Have you been searching for true love everywhere and found none? Do you want the love of God to overflow in your life so that you will become a carrier and giver of love to others? Allow me to show you love that flows from the Throne Room of Grace. I encourage you to read on.

—John Akeem Olukayode Shomade
United Kingdom

Introduce Me to Love

In his book *Questions of Life*, Nicky Gumbel quotes Freud as saying, "People are hungry for love."[2] One of the attributes that makes Jesus so special to me is His love, especially for the loveless—the outcasts, lepers, and prostitutes. Love seems to motivate all that He did. More importantly, His love shown through His death on the cross is the ultimate gift to humankind. He loved His enemies on the cross and pleaded with the Father for their forgiveness, saying "Father, forgive them, for they do not know what they are doing" (Luke 22:34). That's the heart of a real lover. I believe that we all have a room for love in our lives—all we need to do is surrender every part of our being to love and let Jesus embrace and romance us in totality. Allow Him to touch those areas that we have deliberately withheld from Him and He will take us to the places we've never been before.

"God is love" is a theme that resonates in His creation, redemption, and affection towards humanity. He lives inside us (1 John 4:7-12 and John 3:16). It is His love that draws us to Himself. It is because of His love and mercy that we are sustained. Love is our natural inheritance and the essence of our being. Nothing can separate us from the Father's love. From Genesis to Revelation,

---

2   Nicky Gumbel, Questions of Life (Alpha Books, 2011), 28.

we can feel, embrace, and make connection with the love of our heavenly Father as we read from the account of creation to the second coming of Christ. In fact, creation itself shows us the love of our heavenly Father. He created us in His image and likeness and put His spirit inside us so we could have a relationship with Him through worship and our daily fellowship. The more we know Him, the more His love envelopes and transforms us until any contrary nature and lifestyle is deleted and we become like Him.

Creation in the Bible is more than speaking the earth and its inhabitants into being; it also means sustaining and caring for the created. It was the first means by which our heavenly Father expressed his love to our planet. Love in creation is God's way of saying, "I am never remote from the inevitable heartaches of My children." The focus of creation was on humankind (Genesis 2:4-25; Ezekiel 28:12-19), which was God's idea, and marriage is a godly idea that reflects the marriage between Christ and the Church (Ephesians 5:27). Think about it, God, who is not lonely, being served by millions of angels, seeks to have a loving relationship with us. He puts beauty and order into an otherwise disorderly earth as a potter creates a pot out of formless clay.

God created Adam in His image and dealt with him through the eye of love. He felt this wholesome Adam should not be alone. Woman was created from one of his ribs and named Eve (*chauvah* in Hebrew, meaning "life") because she is the mother of all living beings. As God created us in His image, we are all created in love. He has deposited His unconditional love in us.

Love is the heart of Jesus' teaching. He taught us to follow His example by being kind to the ungrateful and to those with evil intent. In Luke 6:35-36, Jesus instructs us to love our enemies, do good to those who hate us, and lend to others without expecting to get anything back. Without love, the above command is practically impossible to obey. It is so important to Jesus that when asked to identify the greatest commandment, He said it was: "Love the Lord with all your heart and with all your mind and with all your strength (Mark 12:30; Matthew 22:37-40).

Through the eyes of love, Jesus willingly embraced the cross. He died for us while we were still sinners—He laid down His life for humankind. His teaching promotes love and mercy. We see an example of His teaching from the parable of the lost son, popularly known as the Prodigal Son. In this parable, after the wayward son had squandered his inheritance, he came to his senses and returned home. The father showed us an example of walking in love by embracing his son as he allowed the outflowing of the divine love that has been shed abroad in his heart by the Holy Spirit (Luke 15:20). This forgiving love of the father symbolizes the divine mercy of God.

Now let's go together to change your image or perception of love forever.

What is This Thing Called Love?

We think and talk a lot about love. We often say things such as "I love you" or "I love to play sports." We also say "I love you" to our family or special friends. If you gather a group of teenagers or children together, and ask them what they understood by *love*, I'm certain you would get a diverse range of answers depending on their mind-set and their environment.

> Very rarely will anyone die for a righteous person, though for a good person someone might possibly dare to die. But God demonstrates his own love for us in this: While we were still sinners, Christ died for us.
>
> (Romans 5:7-8)

Jesus' death on the cross is the hallmark of the Father's divine love for His children. And since we have been made right in God's sight by the blood of Christ, He will certainly save us from God's condemnation.

A group of researchers decided to conduct a study on the meaning of love. They decided to ask some children from age four to eight, "What does love mean to you?" This group must have read Jesus' reply to the chief priest: "And they said to Him, "Do you hear what these are saying?" And Jesus replied to them, "Yes; have you never read, out of the mouths of babes and un-weaned infants you have made (provided) perfect praise?" (Matthew 21:15-17).

The children(s) replies ranged from:

1. "Love is when you go out to eat and give somebody most of your French fries without making them give you any of theirs"

2. "Love is when you tell a guy you like his shirt, and then he wears it every day"

3. "Love is when Mommy gives Daddy the best piece of chicken"

4. "Love is when your puppy licks your face after you left him alone all day"

5. "Love is when my mommy makes coffee for my daddy and she takes a sip before giving it to him, to make sure the taste is OK."

The children's answers above reflect their understanding of love. I think if we asked a group of adults the same question, we would have some really interesting answers, probably in line with the children's understanding but just more sophisticated because the adults would probably include some emotions and adjectives like *affection, soft spot, fondness, a person you cherish, someone you fancy,* and *enjoying being in the presence of someone.* All the above may encompass or have the trapping of some form of love, which will be discussed later in this chapter. However, the above Scripture tells us that God showed us real love by sending Christ to die for us while we were still sinners. This is the hallmark of true love.

Love can take on different meanings depending on the context and the targeted recipient. We use the words *I love you* without really appreciating the effects of our words on the recipient. At times, what we are really saying is, *I like you*. Our love for chocolate has a different meaning to our love for parents; likewise, our love for husband or wife is quite different from that of friends and acquaintances. Jesus admonishes us to love God with all our heart, soul, and mind; and to love our neighbor as ourselves (Matthew 22:37-40). That tells me that love requires real commitment that is not artificial but straight from our heart.

DEFINITIONS OF LOVE

Many people have attempted to define or describe love in their finite way. Here are various attempts to describe love:

1. Jimi Hendrix, the famous American rock guitarist, composer, and singer, stated, "When the power of love overcomes the love of power, the world will know peace."[3] While I may not agree with everything concerning this famous guitarist, I actually agree with this quote as love has been driven out because of our greed and the desire to dominate and control others.

2. One source defines *love* as: "To have a great affection for a person or thing, to have a passionate desire for someone or an intense emotion of affection toward a person."[4]

3. The *Longman Modern English Dictionary* defines love as "A powerful emotion felt for another person manifesting itself in deep affection, devotion or sexual desire." This tells us

---

3   Jimi Hendrix, BrainyQuote, https://www.brainyquote.com/quotes/quotes/j/jimihendri195397.html.

4   *Collins Concise Dictionary & Thesaurus*, 3rd ed. (2003).

that to love someone is to hold that person dear in our heart, to appreciate people, to cherish them, dote on them, have affection for them, and to be in a deep emotional relationship with them. We shall explore the different meanings of love in the latter part of this book.

The above are good attempts to describe love, but not the whole story. While love includes all the above, it goes beyond a gentle smile, or a warm and tender touch. In fact, it is impossible to fully describe God, so it is impossible for our finite mind to find words to really describe love. Everything that I am about to say is merely an attempt.

One of the most powerful descriptions of love in the Bible is found in 1 Corinthians 13:1-13, where Paul made a very bold and sound description of love.

If I speak in the tongues of men and of angels, but have not love, I am only a resounding gong or a clanging cymbal. If I have the gift of prophecy and can fathom all mysteries and all knowledge, and if I have a faith that can move mountains, but have not love, I am nothing. If I give all I possess to the poor and surrender my body to the flames, but have not love, I gain nothing.

Love is patient, love is kind. It does not envy, it does not boast, it is not proud. It is not rude, it is not self-seeking, it is not easily angered, and it keeps no record of wrongs. Love does not delight in evil but rejoices with the truth. It always protects, always trusts, always hopes, and always perseveres.

Love never fails. But where there are prophecies, they will cease; where there are tongues, they will be stilled;

where there is knowledge, it will pass away. For we know in part and we prophesy in part. But when perfection comes, the imperfect disappears. When I was a child, I talked like a child, I thought like a child, I reasoned like a child. When I became a man, I put childish ways behind me. Now we see but a poor reflection as in a mirror; then we shall see face to face. Now I know in part; then I shall know fully, even as I am fully known.

And now these three remain: faith, hope and love. But the greatest of these is love.

Love bears up under anything and everything, and it is always ready to believe the best of every person. Its hopes are fadeless under all circumstances and it endures everything (without weakening). Love never fails, never fades out or becomes obsolete or comes to an end (verses 7-8). Love never fails. That is, when you live by love, you cannot fail. Nothing works without it, and there can be no failure with it. It takes faith to believe that love will not fail. The natural man and his world are ruled by selfishness. When you practice love by faith and refuse to seek your own, you put the Father into action on your behalf. Walking in love is to your great advantage and agape love is a new kind of power that makes you master of every situation. Love is truly the only sure secret of our success.

This is what love is like, and Christians are to make a concerted effort to take a good spiritual note by God's grace. What unbelievers need is the manifestation of God's love in the Christian's life. They need to know that God is waiting to lavish His love on His children, not because we deserve it but because He made us in His image and likeness, and as such He is besotted with us. Despite his total affection for us, He does not force himself on us. Like Adam and Eve, we have the free will to choose, to trust Him and reciprocate His love. We need to walk the walk and not just talk the talk. Those who come to Him do so in response to His love. Jesus, who is love Himself, went about doing good to everyone without partiality, and humbled Himself without complaint. God has given those who receive His Son, Jesus, as their personal Savior from sin the ability to love as He does, through the power of the Holy Spirit (John 1:12; 3:1, 23-24). In fact, love is the greatest thing (1 Corinthians 13:13).

THE FOUR CATEGORIES OF LOVE

In his book *The Four Loves*, C. S. Lewis divides human love into many different categories. My focus here will be on the four categories that are mentioned in my first book "The Fear Factor" and as used in the Greek tradition (and which therefore appear in the New Testament Scriptures).

1. STORGE (PRONOUNCED STOR-GAY)

This describes affection between members of a family, for example between parents and children. Parental love is the first love a child experiences and the first love he or she understands. It is the one that makes a tired parent stay up all night rocking the child to sleep before they sleep themselves. When there is an affirmation of parent's love, it provides a sense of security and emotional stability. A mother's first love emphases intimacy while a father's first love emphasizes identity. In fact, parental love is often the means by which children actually open themselves up to God's love and come to understand it early in life. This love can also be extended toward non-family members—the main criterion is a comfortable familiarity with the person because we have known them for a long time and are fond of them or something about them. In short, *storge* is a deep and abiding affection.

This type of affection is usually expressed in a comfortable, private, and quiet context. These people provide us with a large share of our happiness on this earth, but we need to guard against misusing our affections to overwhelm the recipient to the extent that love turns into hate. In one of her books, Stormie Omartian suggests that from the time our children are born, we should pray, "God help me to really love my child the way you want me to and teach me how to show it in a way he (or she) can understand." I say a resounding amen to that prayer.

2. PHILIA (PRONOUNCED FEE-LEE-AH)

The word *philia* (dutiful friendship or affection) in Greek is more naturally used to describe intimate affection that is not sexual in nature. Philia always implies an element of preference or favor. Quite naturally, it is especially used for the love of close friends. It often reflects the idea of helping or assisting someone greatly admired. Philia is the embodiment of everything a true, meaningful friendship represents. It is used in John 11, verses 3 and 36, to give us an indication of how deeply Jesus loved Lazarus. Jesus' love was so evident that the Jews had to comment, "See how he loved him!" (John 11:36). Jesus revealed His love for Lazarus by raising him from the position of defeat (death) and giving him a new lease of life. We also see Jesus' love (philia) for humankind revealed through His countless acts of compassionate healing. Examples may be found in Mark 1:41 (healing a man with leprosy) and in Luke 7:13-14, where Jesus raises a widow's son from the dead.

While lovers are normally absorbed face-to-face in each other, and friends live side by side and are absorbed in some common interest, God is *eternally* absorbed in and with us. Philia is the least natural of the loves, the least instinctive, organic, or biological and the least necessary because we can live and breed without friendship. That is one of the reasons friendship love is the least appreciated in our modern society. Two people who fall in love and are sexually active may become friends, as well as lovers, because they have discovered a common interest they share with one another that is not rooted in erotic love. C. S. Lewis, the Irish theologian and Christian apologist, believes the pleasure of friendship is greatest when each brings out all that is best, wisest, and/or funniest in others. But he warns against people joining together for reasons other than shared interests, as this creates elite groups and may cause others to rush to join a group because of the fear of being left outside. This in turn may destroy the original foundation of the friendship. While philia plays a significant role in the Christian experience, agape love is where the primary essence of the love of God can be found.

3. AGAPE (PRONOUNCED AH-GAH-PAY)

The word *agape* in Greek expresses the highest and noblest form of love that sees something infinitely precious in its object. It is a selfless love for others. The old word for agape in English was *charity*, but the Greek meaning captures this type of love more accurately. This is the kind of love one has toward God. It is a kind of love God has for us and is good in all circumstances. It is the kind of love that made Moses put himself on the firing line with the people when God refuses to forgive the people of Israel in Exodus 32.

This is the essence of what Paul wrote in 1 Corinthians13:13 when he said, "Now abide faith, hope, love, these three; but the greatest of these is love." In the New Testament, Jesus gives us the two greatest commandments, "Love the Lord your God with all your heart," and "Love your neighbor as yourself" (Mark 12:30-31).

The word for love in both commandments is a verb based on *agape*. This type of love is not based on feelings but on the will. We make a conscious decision to love, irrespective of any unpleasant actions or reactions from others. It is the kind of love that makes you wish the best for someone and act accordingly, and even toward a person you dislike. *Agape* love helps us to reverse negative feelings to positive ones—for example, if we inadvertently help someone we do not like, we tend to dislike them less.

God is agape, and agape is not feeling. We sometimes confuse Jesus' commandment to love our neighbor in Mark 12:31 with kindness or love for humanity. Kindness is the quality of being friendly, generous and considerate. It desires to relieve another person's suffering whilst love is the willingness of one person to sacrifice a great deal in order to relieve another's suffering. Love for humanity is not the main focus of His commandment because it does not surprise you with inconvenient demands and it does not turn up at your doorstep, stinking and begging. What we love with agape can only be a person, who is real, because a person is the image of God.

Agape is the key to all successful relationships. It was this sacrificial and unconditional love that enabled the Father to sacrifice His only Son for our sinful world. Romans 5:8 tells us, "But God shows and clearly proves His (own) love for us by the fact that while we were still sinners, Christ (the Messiah, the Anointed One) died for us" (AMP).

Agape is all giving without seeking a return. God's love is higher, deeper, truer, and based on self-giving. Its value increases with the passing of time as we go deeper in our walk with God. The Christian alone can grasp and experience all it means. Anyone is capable of eros (passionate emotion); but the redeemed alone love with agape. And it all grows out of God's great love for us, from His grace alone.

John, "the disciple Jesus loved," declared that "God is love" and that God is "agape love" (1 John 4:8, 16). Jesus' followers will be known by their agape love and not for their theology, because you can know all the interpretation of the Scriptures without the love of Jesus in your heart.

4. EROS (PRONOUNCED EH-ROS)

Eros (passionate emotion) describes a romantic love between people who are *in love*. It is the kind of love that exists between husband and wife, and it is sexual in nature. It is usually based on feelings and extends beyond friendship and affection. Eros is the desire to draw out all that is good, beautiful, and true.

Anders Nygren made three observations about eros using the life of Pluto.[5] First, eros is the "love of desire" or acquisitive love manifesting itself as a desire, longing, and striving for what we do not have. Second, eros is our way to the Divine, and people love in the eros sense because they want to get to where the happy gods are and thus be completely satisfied. Third, eros is egocentric love that is utterly human centered. Everything, absolutely everything, revolves around the individual and its self-centered quest for the highest happiness.

---

5   Cited in Lewis A. Drummond, *Love, the Greatest Thing in the World* (Kregel Publications, 1998), 59.

Without eros, none of us would have been born; and without affection none of us would have been reared. Eros love enables lovers to be deeply absorbed in each other, exploring the work of a very creative God. For a biblical picture of erotic love, you need to go no further than the Song of Solomon.

It is important to note that God calls us to meet our spouse's love needs and to consider the needs of "the other half" as being more important than our own. When we do this wholeheartedly, each loving and focusing on meeting the legitimate needs of the other, the relationship is strengthened, and we are winning in our desire to build a strong foundation for a great marriage.

I strongly urge any couples reading this book not to use sex as a weapon to punish your partners. If you do this, you run the risk of losing your spouse to another man or woman, another project, or simply to your children because the love vacuum unwittingly created will need to be filled by someone or something else. By meeting your partner's love needs, you are also strengthening your marriage against temptation.

Eros love may cause emotional attachment, jealousy, an unimaginable level of happiness, and a state of bliss for a short period, which may quickly fade away if it is not accompanied by affection and friendship. In its negative form, eros love may seek to conquer, possess, or use whatever tools possible to achieve a pleasurable moment. It is sometimes demanding and always in a hurry.

True love demands that we offer to our spouse the following: unconditional love and acceptance, sexual intimacy, spiritual intimacy, emotional intimacy and communication, companionship, encouragement, and affirmation. Love goes beyond feelings. It is a deep affection that drives us to care profoundly for someone else. It is also a commitment to act and to actively pursue the best for our loved ones. It involves self-sacrifice irrespective of our feelings and emotions.

According to Jay E. Adams[6], one definition of love based on the biblical teaching is: "The fulfilment of God's commandments, a responsible relationship to God and to man." Adams goes on to say that love is a relationship conditioned by responsibility—that is, responsible observance of the commandments of God.

A FEW COMPARISONS

In Christian theology, the principle of God's action and our response is paramount as we have been taught to recognize that God is always willing to fulfill His plan for us, but He wants to work in partnership with us. Of the words used in Greek for "love," neither philia (dutiful friendship or affection) nor eros (passionate emotion) is adequate to the Christian concept, which the New Testament expresses as agape.

The word is believed to have been coined by the sacred authors from the verb *agapao* to avoid the sensual associations of the ordinary Greek noun eros. It is used only twice in the synoptic Gospels (Matthew 24:12 and Luke 11:42), but often in the book of John and the Pauline epistles (especially 1 Corinthians 13) and Johannine epistles, and always in the context of the love of God or Christ, or of the love of Christians for one another.

In his first encyclical letter, released on 25 December 2005 and titled "Deus Caritas Est," which is Latin for "God is love," Pope Benedict discussed agape love versus eros, with agape love and eros as ascending and descending love that need to find unity

---

6   Jay E. Adams, Competent to counsel: An introduction to Nouthetic Counseling, 2009.

in the one reality of love. Eros and agape—ascending love and descending love—can never be completely separated. The more the two, in their different aspects, find a proper unity in the one reality of love, the more the true nature of love in general is realized. Even if eros is at first mainly covetous and ascending, a fascination for the great promise of happiness in drawing near to the other, it is less and less concerned with itself, and increasingly seeks the happiness of the other. At this stage, eros is concerned more and more with the beloved and releases itself to "be there for" the other. The element of agape thus enters into this love, for otherwise eros is impoverished and even loses its own nature.

On the other hand, we cannot live by this Christian offering of descending love alone. Anyone who wishes to give love must also learn to receive love as a gift. Certainly, as the Lord tells us, one can become a source from which rivers of living water flow (John 7:37-38). Yet to become such a source, one must constantly drink anew from the original source, which is Jesus Christ, from whose pierced heart flows the love of God (John 19:34).

When I think of all this, I fall to my knees and pray to the Father, the Creator of everything in heaven and on earth. I pray that from his glorious, unlimited resources he will empower you with inner strength through his Spirit. Then Christ will make his home in your hearts as you trust in him. Your roots will grow down into God's love and keep you strong. And may you have the power to understand, as all God's people should, how wide, how long, how high, and how deep his love is. May you experience the love of Christ, though it is too great to understand fully. Then you will be made complete with all the fullness of life and power that comes from God. Now all glory to God, who is able, through his mighty power at work within us, to accomplish infinitely more than we might ask or think. Glory to him in the church and in Christ Jesus through all generations forever and ever! Amen.   (Ephesians 3:14-21 NLT)

Like the apostle Paul, one of my utmost desires is that all believers will grow spiritually and know the full extent of God's love and be an infectious carrier of such selfless love to their immediate environment and to the world at large.

PRAYER

Lord, Your Word says that Your love is already inside me because it has been shed abroad in my heart (Romans 5:5). *So today, I resolve to remove every obstacle that would keep that love from flowing freely from me into the lives of others. I put resentments behind me, and I wholeheartedly forgive all those who have done me wrong.*

A Recipe for Love

I received the inspiration for this chapter in the year 2006 during one of my regular fellowship times with a dear friend of mine, Nigel Armstrong, who is a minister of God and a well-known and respectable butcher in the City of London. At the sight of the Meat and Livestock Commission's letter titled "The Recipe for Love," my mind started flowing with the inspiration of writing a chapter with the above title but with my focus not on meat and perishable things, but on the imperishable things. We are talking about the word that makes young boys and girls do crazy things and turn an old man or woman to revisit their teenage years. This word is *love*. The chapter "What is Love?" has laid a good foundation to follow in describing love, in its various forms and characteristics.

We all have the capacity to specialize in giving and receiving love. If you are already walking in love, you could learn to be more perfect in love because "perfect love casts out fear" (1 John 4:18 NASB). Love, if handled sensitively, could make our world a better place to dwell in. In this chapter, you will discover some of the key ingredients in a recipe for love, and how to walk in it.

What is a recipe? It's a "list of ingredients and directions for making a particular dish," or a "formula, method, modus operandi, prescription, procedure, process, programme, or technique."[7] While the Meat and Livestock Commission have their cooking instructions to guide the world's meat consuming population on how to cook pork chops, Provençale, or beef with mustard, I would like to explore the ingredients or recipe for a lasting love.

During my research for this book, I came across the recipes below and I hope that they put a smile on your face and change your view of love for the better. If you look at them with a spiritual insight, they may become simple but effective resources for enriching your love life.

1. "HARRY CONNICK, JR., "RECIPE FOR LOVE"

A little bit of me and a whole lot of you
Add a dash of starlight and a dozen roses, too
Then let it rise for a hundred years or two
And that's the recipe for making love

It doesn't need sugar cause it's already sweet
It doesn't need an oven cause it's got a lot of heat
Just add a dash of kisses to make it all complete
And that's the recipe for making love ………….

2. RECIPE FOR LOVE INGREDIENTS

2 Hearts Full of Love
2 Heaping Cups of Kindness
2 Armfuls of Gentleness
2 Cups of Friendship
2 Cups of Joy
2 Big Hearts Full of Forgiveness

---

7   *Collins Concise Dictionary & Thesaurus*, 3rd ed. (2003).

1 Lifetime of Togetherness
2 Minds Full of Tenderness

Method: Stir daily with Happiness, Humor, and Patience. Serve with Warmth and Compassion, Respect, and Loyalty.

—Author Unknown

3. ANOTHER RECIPE FOR LOVE INGREDIENTS

½ a cup of Affection
A pinch of cuddles
3 tablespoons of pure sweetness
A great big kiss

Method: Dim the lights, then mix them very slowly together.

—Author Unknown

Those are some recipe nuggets for friendship, family, and the erotic kind of love. I do hope it puts a little smile on your face! Some say that love is a dream and cannot be touched. Yet, others declare that love is part of our everyday lives— we breathe, caress, and celebrate love daily. I put it to all my readers that love can really be felt, touched, and caressed daily because love is a reality of our being. In fact, we have all been programmed with the ability to love by our Creator. You can be the recipient or giver of love in your environment. Love is part of your DNA. We need a mixture of suggestions by the authors above because love is not a formula. Love has a way of revealing itself to people in different dimensions and touching places that have previously been left untouched. Love always takes its lovers into a new dimension in life.

Some people are already walking in love while others need to tap deeply into their heart in order to activate it. Love is the greatest gift to humankind from the divine Creator, who is love Himself.

THE ONLY COMMANDMENT

Jesus said, "My command is this: Love each other as I have loved you. Greater love has no one than this: to lay down one's life for one's friends" (John 15:12-13).

God is love. It is so important to Jesus that when He was asked to identify the greatest commandment, He said it was to "Love the Lord your God with all your heart and with all your soul and with all your mind and with all your strength" (Mark 12:30; Matthew 22:37-40). Simply put, those who have interest in Christ ought to love one another, and if you expect the benefit of God's compassion towards you, be compassionate one to another. We must interest ourselves in the concerns of others in Christian love and sympathy and let no one be selfish but think about others. A selfish spirit is destructive to the operation and manifestation of Christian love (Philippians 2:4).

Love is the heart of Jesus' teaching. He teaches us to follow His example by being kind to the ungrateful and to those with evil intent. In Luke 6:35-36, Jesus instructs us to love our enemies, do good to them, and lend to them without expecting to get anything back.

BURDEN BEARING
AND THE LAW OF CHRIST

The main point of Galatians 6:1-5 is given in a general way (in verse 2) and a specific way before in verse 1. Verse 2 says,

"Bear one another's burdens, and so fulfill the law of Christ." If a Christian brother or sister is weighed down or menaced by some burden or threat, be alert to that and quickly do something to help. Don't let them be crushed. Don't let them be destroyed. Don't be like the scribes and Pharisees. Jesus said, "They tie up heavy, cumbersome loads and put them on other people's shoulders, but they themselves are not willing to lift a finger to move them" (Matthew 23:4).

Don't increase burdens; instead make them lighter for people.

Some readers may wonder what you are supposed to do with your life. Here is a vocation that will bring you more satisfaction than if you became a billionaire ten times over. Develop the extraordinary skill for detecting the burdens of others and devote yourself daily to making them lighter. It does not have to be a big thing—a smile or empathizing with someone hurting is good enough. That is showing the love of God.

"Carry each other's burdens, and in this way you will fulfill the law of Christ" (Galatians 6:2). That's an interesting directive in a book that declares in Galatians 5:18: "If you are led by the Spirit you are *not* under the law." And in Galatians 3:13: "Christ redeemed us from the curse of the law." Have we been freed from the curse and burden of the Mosaic law just to be burdened down with a more radical law of Christ? No. The difference is that Moses gave us the law but could not change our hearts so that we would freely obey. Our pride and rebellion was not conquered by Moses.

But when Christ summons us to obey His law of love, He offers us Himself to slay the dragon of our pride, change our hearts, empower us by His Spirit, and fulfil His law. That is why, even though Christ's law is more radical than the righteousness of the scribes and Pharisees, He can say, "Come to me, all who labor and are heavy-laden, and I will give you rest. Take my yoke upon you and learn from me; for I am gentle and lowly in heart, and you will find rest for your souls. For my yoke is easy, and my burden is light" (Matthew 11:28-30).

The law of Christ is not easily fulfilled in the flesh because it is excessively pleasant or tolerant. It is, however, easy because when we are weak, He is strong. It is easy because He produces the fruit of love: "I have been crucified with Christ and I no longer live, but Christ lives in me. The life I now live in the body, I live by faith in the Son of God, who loved me and gave himself for me" (Galatians 2:20 NIV).

Christ never commands us to do anything that He wants us to do on our own or by our power. Therefore, every command in the law of Christ is a call to faith. Through *faith* God supplies the Spirit of Christ (Galatians 3:5); through the *Spirit* we produce the fruit of love (5:22); through *love* we fulfill the *law* of Christ (6:2). Therefore, if you *trust* Him, you will fulfill His law of love. You will devote yourself to lifting the burdens of others.

PRAYER

In Jesus' name, I make a fresh commitment today to live the life of love, to let the tenderness of God flow through me and heal the wounded hearts of those I meet.

His Compassionate Love Heals

'Love Heals' by Jonathan Larson, American composer and playwright likens love to the breath of midnight air, a lighthouse, and a prayer that activates healing. The lyrics admonish those who shield their hearts, those who quit before they start, and those who have frozen up the part of them that feels, and assures them that love heals. It continues by encouraging us to hold on to love even when we feel like giving up, as love will keep us strong. Love heals when the pain is too much to bear and when we reach out our hand, and only the wind is there. When we feel that life's unfair and when we feel so small, like a grain of sand, there we would find the healing hand of love. When we fear the storm ahead and lie awake in bed alone with no one there to stroke our head, don't forget love heals. Love ... heals!

I am a believer in the power of love to heal because I've seen the suffering caused by lack of love or perceived lack of affection. I have seen a young person who previously suffered from chronic character flaws changed to become the most polite, well-mannered, and pleasant human being because of the presence of love. I have seen people divorced and very bitter for a long time subsequently become very likeable and lovable after restoration of love. Some people had given up on love or the marriage thing, even publicly attacked a necessity for marriage, but change their mind when love came into their lives, to the extent they became spokespersons for marriage. I know love heals and agree with Jonathon Larson that love heals.

COMPASSIONATE HEALING ON THE SABBATH

We were introduced to another aspect of compassionate healing that exposes the dogmatic heart of the spiritual rulers of the day.

On a Sabbath Jesus was teaching in one of the synagogues, and a woman was there who had been crippled by a spirit for eighteen years. She was bent over and could not straighten up at all. When Jesus saw her, he called her forward and said to her, "Woman, you are set free from your infirmity." Then he put his hands on her, and immediately she straightened up and praised God.

Indignant because Jesus had healed on the Sabbath, the synagogue leader said to the people, "There are six days for work. So come and be healed on those days, not on the Sabbath."

The Lord answered him, "You hypocrites! Doesn't each of you on the Sabbath untie your ox or donkey from the stall and lead it out to give it water? Then should not this woman, a daughter of Abraham, whom Satan has kept bound for eighteen long years, be set free on the Sabbath day from what bound her?"

When he said this, all his opponents were humiliated, but the people were delighted with all the wonderful things he was doing.   (Luke 13:10-17)

The Sabbath, the seventh day of the week, is set aside for the worship of God and for rest. One of the most important of Jewish laws was keeping the Sabbath holy. This meant that the Sabbath day was to be kept as a true day of rest and also a joyous day of celebration. Yet, as Jewish laws were continuously interpreted and thus expanded, the rules for the Sabbath became more edicts of what not to do, rather than guiding principles for the preservation of the one day when people could put aside the toils of daily obligations and come together in the sacred bonds of family and friends. By his words and actions Jesus rescued the Sabbath from dull conformity and returned it to a day of joyful celebration.

We can become obsessed with the enforcement of rules and lose sight of the purpose of rules. When we look at the rules society at large sets before us, we must place them in the light of Jesus' ministry. What Jesus did was not merely to give a liberal interpretation of the laws of his religion or society. He was not saying that people can decide for themselves what they do on the Sabbath. Rather, He was reminding them of the true meaning and purpose of the tradition. He transformed the traditions of his day and enlightened the limited vision of the people to engage them in the hopeful dimensions of the kingdom of God.

It is always God's will to heal the sick. Jesus had compassion on the woman bent over for 18 years and out of His love for humankind risked the wrath of the religious leaders. He set free those who were in bondage to evil powers, thus implicitly subverting economic, political, and even religious structures and guiding rules to deal with such issues, even though the people involved in this process might not have thought in these terms. Jesus offered something to them that society would not—that is, love, acceptance, respect, and an equal place and voice.

The woman in Luke's story, crippled and bent over, is restored to the Abrahamic covenant of good health through the loving touch and decree of Jesus. He understood that she was an "outsider," not just by virtue of her physical ailment, but by her gender, period! She was a woman. Here Jesus broke the bonds of Jewish legalism and society's prejudices, and restored this woman to her rightful place as an equal beneficiary in her society.

Liberation is a sign of God's power and mercy. It is only through the love of God that we can truly be liberated from those attitudes and actions that hinder our relationship to others and God. When we truly abide by the commandments of Jesus, to love one another and to love God, then we will find ourselves released from the limited powers of our own ways of understanding and restored to a peace found only in a right relationship with God, and thus we will find that we enjoy that same peaceful relationship with others. Such relationships are formed through love, trust, respect, and forgiveness.

The healing of the woman and the restoration of a wayward Hebrew people are the stories of God's radical love for us. God loves us precisely because we are imperfect; the problem is, we can't find it within ourselves to love ourselves and others through our imperfections. The suffering of the bent-over woman would not have miraculously ended with her healing by Jesus. The suffering of the wandering Hebrews would not have ended with their return to their promised land. Instead, their suffering was transformed by the presence of divine compassion, charity, or love into an inexplicable consolation and comfort.

Jesus empathizes with the suffering of this woman, and all those who came to him for help, perhaps fully realizing what lay ahead for Him. Jesus brought the compassion of a suffering God to bear on the reality of the human condition, offering the hope of compassionate consolation despite unchangeable circumstances and overwhelming odds.

The God exhibited through the actions of Jesus Christ is indeed a suffering God, a God whose power is interwoven with pain to reveal to us the highest excellence of love, the deepest essence of compassionate love. The mystery of God is here in solidarity with those who suffer.

The compassionate love of Jesus releases the woman doubled over from the infirmity of the human perspective of her limitations, and opens her to the possibilities of her authenticity as a sacred bearer of God's image, as one of God's holy creations. The healing of the doubled-over woman is more figurative than it is literal. If we read the Greek text closely, we find that the usual word for "healing" does not appear. Instead, we find a word that is usually translated as "to release" or "to send away." Basically, Jesus is freeing this woman from her bondage; He is releasing her from a force that has kept her captive.

Jesus teaches us that there is no room in the kingdom of God for social oppression and religious legalism that bind us to unhealthy views of each other based on how we were born into this world. The power found through the kingdom of God is not a power of domination but a power of responsible love that effects transformation; it is a power that enables the freedom and autonomy of others, that empowers us to engage in gentle persuasion, and imparts through us patient love and encouragement.

Jesus heals the woman to be His helper or messenger, the one with a renewed physical ability to carry forth His message. This is how the kingdom of God works—made visible and understandable to humanity through those of us willing to claim the call of Christ. The kingdom of God is not realized through the human appearance of an omnipotent God. Rather, it is achieved through disciples who are willing, despite the costs, to accept our human condition with fundamental faith in God's compassionate love.

LOVE IN ACTION

"When he saw the crowds, he had compassion on them, because they were harassed and helpless, like sheep without a shepherd."   (Matthew 9:36)

Compassion is a deep yearning that responds to the needs of people. It is much deeper than sympathy. Sympathy can just sit around feeling sorry for people. Compassion has to do with doing something for the hurting. Jesus is always at work because His Father never stops working on our behalf. In other words, compassion equates love for the afflicted.

Compassionate love is what motivates God, and Jesus' life on earth was a picture of that love in action. His whole ministry was driven by it. It was this love that caused Him to multiply the loaves and fishes, heal the sick, cast out demons, and raise the dead. It was love for us that compelled Him to go to the cross. And it is that same love that He now longs to pour out through us. His love compels us to cast out demons and set the captives free. He is really the Lover that heals. He wants us to move in the same compassionate love towards our fellow human beings, which motivates us to pray for the sick, birthing a desire to banish suffering and meet the needs of others. We need to follow Jesus' example by spending more time in fellowship with our Father, and meditate on His love until it rises up strong on the inside of us.

PERSONAL TESTIMONY

I recently had a biopsy to investigate the presence of prostate cancer, and not only was the procedure painful to me, but I also had an E-coli urinary tract infection that would not disappear despite using different types of antibiotics until the correct one was identified via a urine sample. I was in severe pain and troubled, with discomfort at a level unknown to me previously. In addition, I suffered significant lower urinary tract symptoms with frequency, urgency, and a slightly reduced flow rate.

The first two weeks were really bad as the pain became my acquaintance and I was losing weight fast because I could not eat. My only sources of sustenance were soup and liquids, as my tongue felt like poison. By the third week, I told some friends and family, and there I witnessed the wheel of compassion moving with prayers being offered to God on my behalf from many areas, some of which I do not know. Some called every day to pray for and with me, while others visited and yet others just prayed in their respective homes. The compassionate love of God motivated brothers and sisters in Christ into action.

I finally got the result of the biopsy, which stated one out of the twelve samples taken had low traces of nonaggressive prostate cancer. Prayer will continue until all traces of cancer leave my body, because it is a "stranger that must come out of its hiding places and fade away into its extinction" (Psalm 18:45). And besides, my body is a temple of the Holy Spirit; therefore, any form of cancer is disallowed and evicted with immediate effect. Why? Jesus himself took my infirmities and bore my sickness in His body and nailed it all on the cross (Matthew 8:17), and with His stripes I was healed (Isaiah 53:5). As I write now, all traces of prostate cancer have left my body totally—praise the compassionate God that heals (Jesus).

COMPASSIONATE LOVE THAT RESTORES

Lazarus was terribly sick when Martha and Mary sent for Jesus to come. Jesus knew the full extent of the sickness and yet, "When he heard that Lazarus was sick, he stayed where he was two more days" (John 11:6). Here, Jesus gave a hint when He said, "this sickness is for the glory of God" (11:4). He eventually came to set Lazarus free from the bondage of death because of His compassionate love for His friend.

As I dwell upon the compassionate resurrection of Lazarus, I am reminded of the healing of Bartimaeus. This story can be found in Matthew 20, Luke 18, and Mark 10. I figure this story has to be important if it is in the Gospels three times. Bartimaeus was a blind beggar who sat outside Jericho. Growing up, Bartimaeus had surely heard the stories about Jericho's walls crashing down and how great his God was and is. He had faith, and knew God was powerful and able. So, when he hears Jesus is coming through town, he knows he has his chance to be healed.

Studying these passages, and other ones on people being healed, I found a few things of note. First, the people following Jesus were telling him to be quiet when he calls out for Jesus. They do not seem to care about him being healed. This is so different from several other places where friends bring someone in need of healing to Jesus. In Mark 8 another man received healing from blindness, because his friends brought him to Jesus.

In this passage, the people do not seem to think Jesus will heal Bartimaeus. Maybe they had seen him so often by the side of the road, they have written him off as a lost case, but God has a plan. Anyway, Bartimaeus "shouts out all the more," crying for Jesus' mercy. This is why I love reading the Gospels as we get a window into the heart of Jesus. He is so loving, so merciful, and compassionate. He healed the needy, and cried with Mary and Martha when Lazarus died. He is LOVE walking amongst us.

Jesus stops walking. Even though He had somewhere to go (a date with the cross in Jerusalem), He took the time to stop. In Matthew, it says He had compassion for Bartimaeus. In Mark, Jesus asks, "What do you want me to do?" Think about that for a moment. You know that Jesus knows what Bartimaeus wants Him to do. So, why does He ask this question? Because there is power in our words, let us begin to use it effectively. Sometimes it is not enough to believe in our hearts, but we need to speak the word of faith. Jesus healed him, and said, "Your faith has healed you."

Jesus does not always say those words when He heals. So, when He does, I take special note of it. No matter what this man had lived through, no matter the obstacles, no matter the crowds rebuking him, he perseveres and looks to Jesus. He was going to call out to Him. Bartimaeus had called these words: "Son of David, have mercy on me!" He calls Jesus "Son of David," believing He is the Messiah, and crying out for His mercy. What is Jesus' response? First, He encourages the man's faith by having him speak what he wants Him to do, and then He heals him. What a great compassionate God we serve.

Now, what I really love about this story is that Bartimaeus followed Jesus. Not all of the healed do that. Some go back to their homes, to their families, praising God. But blind Bartimaeus follows Jesus. This tells me that our testimonies can cause others to praise and follow Jesus.

PRAYER

Father God, my spirit, body and soul bless Your holy name and praise You. By faith, I activate the anointing to be healed and delivered from every demonic power causing sickness and disease. As You enable me, I promised that by Your help, I will be compassionate to others needing healing. I don't want to ever rebuke anyone for seeking Your mercy. Lord, forgive me for times I have been judgmental to others. Let me always confess with my words who You are and what You can do. Help me always to remember to praise You and follow You and lead others to You! In Jesus' name I pray, amen.

Teach Me How to Forgive

Forgiveness is the act of pardoning, exonerating, or showing clemency or mercy to an offender. However, psychologists generally define forgiveness as a conscious, deliberate decision to release feelings of resentment or vengeance toward a person or group who has harmed us, regardless of whether they actually deserve it. Forgiveness is not an emotion; it is a conscious decision we all make to release others though they may have hurt us. Forgiveness is not forgetting. It does not mean tolerating sin, nor does forgiveness seek revenge or demand repayment. It simply means leaving justice up to God, who said, "Vengeance is mine, I will repay" (Romans 12:1 NASB).

On the cross, Jesus was wounded for our transgressions and was bruised for our iniquities (Isaiah 53:5). He paid the price for all our sins. He did this so that we might have peace with God through forgiveness. In Psalm 32:1-2, the Psalmist assures us that "blessed is he whose transgressions are forgiven, whose sins are covered. Blessed is the man whose sin the Lord does not count against him and in whose spirit is no deceit." This is the kind of forgiveness we need and can receive from God. All of us without exception need forgiveness from God, and Jesus, through His act of love on the cross, provided the platform for our forgiveness so that whosoever confesses Him as Lord and Savior receives the full reconciliation with the Father. "If we confess our sins, He is faithful and righteous to forgive us our sins and cleanse us from all unrighteousness" (1 John 1:9 NASB).

In the Sermon on the Mount, Jesus taught us to pray, "Forgive us our debts [trespasses], as we have forgiven our debtors," that is, those who trespass against us (Matthew 6:12). It simply means that if we forgive others, God will forgive us. Many Christians do not receive answers to their prayers because they fail to forgive others. Unforgiveness is a common problem that blocks people's spiritual lives, and many do not know it.

If we fail to forgive, it leads to some disruptive consequences such as bitterness, strife, disharmony, malice, contention, hatred, and war. However, the results that flow from forgiveness include: reconciliation, peace, harmony, understanding, and fellowship.

ESCAPING THE CURSE

To obtain release from a curse, one of the main requirements is to confess any known sin committed by ourselves and our ancestors, for at times it is the sin of ancestors that exposed us to the curse. To escape from the curse, we need to deal with the sin that exposed us to that curse. How do we achieve this? By confessing the sin and asking God to forgive and cleanse us from the resultant unrighteousness. "He who covers his sins will not prosper, but whoever confesses and forsakes them will have mercy" (Proverbs 28:13 NKJV). Covering our sins may lead to lack of prosperity and could stand as an obstacle against prayers. However, by confessing them we receive God's mercy and redemption from the curse.

HEALING IN FORGIVENESS

"Have you rejected Judah completely? Do you despise Zion? Why have you afflicted us so that we cannot be healed? We hoped for peace but no good has come, for a time of healing but there is only terror" (Jeremiah 14:19). We are also admonished to forgive quickly so that our soul, mind, body, and health might be spared (Proverbs 10:22). It means unforgiveness may delay our wholeness (both spiritual and physical) and we are the architect of it all. Before expounding on the above Scriptures, I would like to share a story.

STORY (AUTHOR UNKNOWN)

Once upon a time in the USA, there was a generous, loyal man who was an excellent provider for his wife and children. Unfortunately, the wife was having an office romance and in love with another man. At the divorce hearing, the wife was awarded custody of the children and she moved to another state. The man was filled with pain and bitterness unknown to him previously. The man was brokenhearted and the house was silent and full of memories. Deep depression and murderous rage crept in as a result of his emotional nightmare, and his job performance dipped to an all-time low and his friends withdrew from him.

The man cried for help by going to his pastor friend, and was told to forgive his ex-wife. He flew into rage again at the thought of forgiving her and suffered unnecessarily.

What happens when we don't forgive?

1. You break God's command to "forgive us our debts as we forgive our debtors" (Matthew 6:12-15), meaning if you don't forgive others, you have no ground to expect your heavenly

Father to forgive you. Simply put, the command is given for your benefit.

2. Forgiveness is necessary to avoid giving Satan the legal ground of afflicting your life (2 Corinthians 2:11), for he uses your inability to forgive as a yardstick to block your relationship with God. Now consider someone who has offended you lately that you refused to forgive. What's the effect of your decision on your peace and freedom?

3. Refusal to forgive others usually condemns you to a lifetime sentence in emotional prison because the offence is going to hold the key to your peace. You will be tormented by Satan until you forgive. Why not allow Jehovah Shalom (God of our peace) take you to the place of peace and tranquility?

4. You prevent yourself from the place of complete healing and freedom, and become bitter instead of getting better (Proverbs 14:10). When bitterness gets into your soul, you begin the death process instead of allowing the peace of God that surpasses all understanding to radiate throughout your mind and soul, giving you life (Philippians 4:7).

5. You prevent yourself from attaining the desire of most believers, becoming Christlike, when you do not forgive. The apostle Paul wrote: "Let all bitterness and wrath and anger and clamor and slander be put away from you, along with all malice. And be kind to one another, tender-hearted, forgiving each other, just as God in Christ also has forgiven you" (Ephesians 3:31-32).

STEPS TO FORGIVENESS

These steps can help you to walk through the process of forgiving others from your heart and to unchain yourself from past hurt.

1. Ask God to reveal to your mind the people you need to forgive. Write their names down. It may surprise you that at the top of that list are your close relatives, your friends, your spouse—and possibly your pastor and church. However, we tend to leave out self and God. We need to forgive ourselves for sin committed through those moments of weakness. And sometimes we are bitter towards God because we hold false expectations of Him. We need to release ourselves and God from those false expectations in order to appropriate God's forgiveness.

2. Acknowledge that you are hurting. Work through your list of people and start the process of forgiveness by stating specifically what you are forgiving them for (rejection, injustice, deprivation of love, sexual or emotional abuse, betrayal, neglect, etc.)

3. Place all situations under the cross. At the cross Christ makes forgiveness legally and morally right. Jesus died for all of our sins "once and for all" (Hebrews 10:10). Ignore the cry of the heart of unfairness or injustice; instead, focus on the full provisions on the cross.

4. Decide not to retaliate now or in the future by using others' sins against them (Luke 6:27-34). Be merciful like your Father, and bear the burden of each person's sin (Galatians 6:1-2). It does not mean that you tolerate sin or obstruct justice by refusing to testify in a court of law, but it is the forgiveness in your heart that really matters to God.

5. Decide to forgive as this is a crisis of the will or a conscious choice to let the other person free in order to free yourself from the past and stop unnecessary pain.

6. Take your list to God and pray for each individual on that list until every pain is specifically addressed. If you are still bitter towards someone, speak to a Christian counsellor or trusted friend to assist you in facilitating the process. You may use words like, "I forgive (name) for _____ (list offences and how they made you feel) and I release (name) from the consequences today with the help of the Holy Spirit in Jesus' name. Amen."

7. Destroy the list and do not tell the offenders what you have done, as this is between you and God. It does not matter if the person is dead or alive; neither does it matter if the person wishes to be reconciled with you. Your freedom in Christ does not and cannot be dependent upon others, whom you have no right or ability to control.

8. Do not expect your decision to forgive others lead to major changes in the other person's attitude towards you; otherwise, you may be setting yourself up for disappointment. Choose to pray for them to find freedom in forgiveness (2 Corinthians 2:7).

9. Try to understand the people you have forgiven, but don't rationalize their behavior as it could lead to an incomplete forgiveness. For example, don't say I forgive my spouse because I know that he or she did not mean it. That would be excusing them and bypassing your pain and the need to forgive from the heart.

TEACH ME HOW TO FORGIVE

10. Expect positive results from forgiveness in you. When forgiveness has taken its root in you, seeing or remembering their offences against you will no longer trigger negative emotions in you. That means you are free from them.

11. Thank God for the lessons you have learnt and the maturity you have gained as a result of the offences and your decision to forgive the offenders (Romans 8:28-29).

12. Accept your part of the blame for the offences suffered. Confess your failure to God (1 John 1:9) and to others (James 5:16) and realize that if someone has something against you, you must go to that person and be reconciled.

NO EXCUSE FOR NOT FORGIVING

In Ephesians 4:32, the apostle Paul encourages us to "be kind to one another, tenderhearted, forgiving one another, even as God in Christ forgave you."

He is very clear about forgiveness: if you will not forgive others, God cannot forgive you. God forgives you, and until you forgive, you will live in torment, and God Himself personally guarantees it.

A perfect example is given in the Bible about the unforgiving servant (Matthew 18:21-35) whereby the king called in a servant who owed him the equivalent of ten million dollars and ordered him to pay up. The servant could not pay back this sum, so the king ordered him and his family to be sold. The servant begged for patience and time to pay it back, and the Bible states that the king was moved with compassion and forgave the entire debt. However, the same servant went out and found a man who owed him the equivalent of twenty dollars, and could not pay his debt. The forgiven servant threw him into prison. The king got to hear about this, and called the servant he forgave and said, "You wicked servant! Should you not have had compassion on the fellow servant, just as I had pity on you?" (Matthew 8:32-33). Then the king, moved with anger, handed him over to torturers.

Like this servant, we have been forgiven by God through the death of His Son, yet we fail to forgive others. Remember, if you will not forgive others, God will not forgive you and then you will be sent to the tormentors. Your prayers become an offence in the sight of God and no one can deliver you. I would like to encourage you to stop being offended right now as it is not God's will for you.

If Christians start to forgive other Christians, I believe a mighty revival will sweep across our land, and it will save marriages and every other relationship and bring the much-needed unity to the body of Christ. The medical community tells us that resentment and bitterness causes heart trouble, high blood pressure, strokes, and other ailments afflicting humankind. It means that we are killing ourselves through the sin of unforgiveness.

CONCLUSION

Forgiveness is not forgetting but the latter could be a product of the former. When God says He will remember our sins no more (Hebrews 10:17), He is not saying, "I will forget them." Rather, He will never use the past against us, as He will remove it as far from us as "the east is from the west" (Psalm 103:12).

To not forgive others is sentencing yourself to living in emotional hell. Perhaps you are hurting from the rejection of parents or a dear friend, or the betrayal of your spouse or business partner, or the emotional devastation of a bitter divorce or sibling separation. And you've allowed resentment to fester in your soul, and bitterness has become your controller. You laugh and your laughter is hollow. You smile, but behind the mask are tears and you go through the motions daily like a robot without feelings, and peace is eluding you.

I'd like to recommend forgiveness as the first step to your healing and freedom. Go through the twelve steps to forgiveness (if needed) but God sometimes sidetracks formulas and goes straight for the heart when your time has come. Be honest with God and cooperate with His leading. I urge you today to "take the medicine of forgiveness." Do it quickly and receive wholeness—body, soul, and spirit.

PRAYER

Lord Jesus, I thank You for pardon, mercy, and forgiveness. Thank You for forgiving me my sins, transgressions, and mistakes. Your peace and joy are filling me up as evidence that my record is spotless because of your righteousness. Today, I forgive myself and those who have sinned against me, hurt me, and caused me harm in any way. I forgive them without hesitation because You showed me mercy, and the servant is not above his master, and You showed me the template on the cross. Help me to work on developing my character rather than attacking others and to control my tongue so I speak words of discipline, not harsh words of judgment. I will walk in love, and by Your special grace. I will forgive in advance anyone who may wrong me today, in Jesus' name. Amen.

Teach Me to Discipline My Child in Love

Once upon a time there was a clear job description for child-rearing. The parents were well-versed in their parental duties and the children obeyed and respected the wisdom and leadership of their parents, elders, teachers, and the government. In fact, child-rearing was not just a job for the biological parents. The responsibilities spilled over to the extended families, the community parents, the educational parents, societal parents, and even the governmental parents. Everyone worked together to bring up the child in a godly manner because of the operation of love in their midst. The child matured to become a valuable and respectable member of society, who not only respects the godly values but also respects good moral values and also has the fear of God.

By the fear of God, I mean awesome respect, love, and trust to obey His commands. Unlike the way we sometimes obey our earthly fathers, teachers, and those in authority because we fear their punishment, the fear of the Lord simply means obeying Him and His commands. If you love someone, you will obey their instructions. The fear of the Lord should not be triggered by anxiety or intimidation, nor by the endless keeping of rules. It is liberating and not restrictive, because it gives confidence about the true order of the world. The fear of the Lord provides answers to our deepest needs and produces a secure household (Exodus 1:21). It also produces trustworthy and successful leaders who discharge their duties with integrity and honesty (Exodus 18:21). And it results in the enjoyment of our labor, gives favor and blessing from the Lord, and a rewarding life (Psalm 128:1-4).

THE PROBLEM

Child-rearing today has become a political football department with various governments making laws and policies on these important issues. Well-meaning as they are, they also tend to create many unintended problems. The child protection laws and the influence of some overzealous child protection agency staff members and social workers have created new problems that would take years to solve. The activities of these agencies have caused a decadence of values in schools and society at large. Parents are afraid to discipline their child because they do not want social services on their doorstep.

Likewise, teachers are finding it difficult to control their classroom because they cannot apply the appropriate discipline to a disruptive or unruly child. In fact, some of these unruly children appear to be so well-versed in their rights that teachers are threatened with reports to the social services or Childline. The head teachers, too, have to be mindful of the type of sanctions they apply to situations.

This problem is compounded by the exposure to outside influences that promote loose morality through newspapers, magazines, videos (sexually explicit and morally decadent in nature), music channels, and the advent of celebrity lifestyles. Our children now look up to celebrities with loose moral values for inspiration. Illicit sex, drugs, gang affiliation, guns, and violence have now become the acceptable norm. To make matters worse, the once-revered political leaders have fallen prey to dishonest gain; hence we have the final proof that our society's moral discipline is disintegrating fast.

FALSE BELIEFS

Many parents have been led to believe that certain misbehavior and bad attitudes are a normal part of child development, and that their job is to simply coordinate family life to the best of their abilities, hoping all along that, despite what they are currently experiencing, their children will be all right in the end. If you have ever wished it could be different than this, and dreamt of having children who are well behaved, courteous, respectful, and mature, with a genuine care for their siblings and others, then you need to know this is not an impossible dream. But it does not happen by accident as it requires consistent and unrelenting perseverance, patience, and regular reality checks—and all these are possible.

THE SOLUTION

God's Word and prayer, together with the Holy Spirit's help, provide the original manual on child raising, and anyone willing to examine it in its fullness will find that it has never needed updating or improvement. When the Bible is mentioned in relation to child raising today, many people incorrectly assume that it is a vehicle of harshness, primarily because of poor examples of application where the discipline aspects of Scripture were not balanced with the many other directives, like correcting in love.

TOUGH LOVE

> "Train up a child in the way he should go: and when he is
> old, he will not depart from it." (Proverbs 22:6, KJV)

This is an instruction to parents and when it's applied in its entirety, this text of the Bible is perfect and truly bears desirable fruit. It is a beautiful thing to interact with God-fearing (God-respecting) children and to witness their character, image, and behavior reflecting the Lord. Their lives are shaped by God-fearing parents, and, as they learn to independently apply God's ways, they bring a gift of joy to their families and to our Father in heaven.

The Good Book, the Word of God (Bible) written thousands of years ago, provides insight into dealing with the problem of misbehavior. "Chasten your son while there is hope, and do not set your hearts on his destruction" (Proverbs 19:18 NKJV). I believe that we (parents, guardians, society, and government) have a responsibility to attack this cancer in its infancy before it becomes a life-sapping problem. If you see a negative character trait in a young child (or even a baby), correction is paramount. Firm and reasonable discipline or punishment administered in the short term does not kill; rather, it is indiscipline that tends to destroy family joy and societal values, and in the long run it breeds a cancerous destructive environment. If we obey the Word of God and apply the biblical principles by chastening our children when they are young, there is hope for redemption.

Again, the Word of God in Proverbs 13:24 (NKJV) states, "He who spares his rod hates his son, but he who loves him disciplines him promptly." This is very true and it's a sign of parental love that you discipline your child. In today's world, we see little children as young as five years old doing irresponsible things or clearly being rude, and no one dares to correct them for fear of reprisal. At times, we see a frustrated parent trying to instill a reasonable fear of the Lord upon a child; and we look at them with scornful and abusive eyes. We sometimes mislabelled them "child abuser" because they dare not to "spare the rod."

In spite of my believing in reasonable discipline, I believe it is important that our children are protected against child abusers and child molesters. A reasonable smack on the behind or hand or a reasonable punishment or chastisement won't destroy a child; in fact, it instills boundaries, letting the child know that certain behaviors are not acceptable. Any environment lacking in clear and acceptable boundaries is bound to suffer from indiscipline and undermining of authority, thus leading to a fall in standards. I would like you to imagine a football (or soccer) game involving children of various age groups, where there are no rules, boundaries, or any form of control. What do you think is going to occur in that game? I hate to admit it, but injuries, bullying, bad tempers, and general chaos would ensue.

Likewise, child-rearing without reasonable boundaries followed by a resolve to enforce with sanctions or punishment would only lead to disaster. You do not have an equal relationship with your child. You may adore him or her, but you are a parent and not a friend. It is important to listen, applying gentle persuasion, but in the end you are the parent and your decision counts a great deal. Parents should be prepared to say no and not give in to emotional blackmail or manipulation by our little angels. Loving your children includes teaching them important life values and not agreeing to all their requests as it may lead them to develop little or no respect (or value) for anything provided to them because they know another one is just an "ask" away!

The Bible admonishes children not to despise the chastening of the Lord, nor to detest correction (Proverbs 3:11-12). Why? It's because you correct the ones you love and want to see them grow up to become a well-rounded, polite young adults with integrity who will achieve their purpose in life. When you have given up on a child, effectively you are saying they are beyond redemption and left to face the consequences of their ways. I used to tell my children and the people around me that I correct them because of my love and desire to see that all is well with them, but they should really be worried when I become silent and no longer take an interest in what they are doing. The above Scripture (verse 12) settles the discussion by stating, "For whom the Lord loves He corrects, just as a father the son in whom he delights" (NKJV).

THE REWARD OF LISTENING TO CORRECTION

When you listen to correction, your knowledge and wisdom increase because you benefit from the experience of other people. Proverbs 23:24-25 puts it like this, "The father of the righteous shall greatly rejoice: and he that begetteth a wise *child* shall have joy of him. Thy father and thy mother shall be glad, and she that bares thee shall rejoice" (KJV). Our goal is to train our children up in the way they should go so that, when they are adults, they are well equipped to stand on their own, fulfil God's will and purpose for them with joy, and be strong ambassadors for the Lord. This is our calling as parents, and God provides all that we need to succeed. To answer the call requires commitment and sacrifice; it necessitates a willingness to "swim against the tide" and confidently stand on God's fail-proof direction.

Our goal is not just to raise *good* children, because the definition of "good" in this world is left open to interpretation. Rather, our goal is to raise righteous children who are in right standing with

God. Do not be misled into thinking that a child who is well-behaved and spiritually mature equates to an unhappy, repressed child. Instead, the reverse is true. A child who understands and respects boundaries will become comfortable and emotionally secure in that environment, and will exude more consistent happiness because of an absence of bad behavior and destructive attitudes.

LESSONS FROM THE BIBLE

In 1 Samuel 2:12 to the end of chapter 3, we find a situation whereby a very respected, anointed, and influential prophet of God (Eli) failed to discipline his two children (Hopni and Phinehas). The two sons caused misery to the people of God, dishonored women who came to the house of God, and despised the offering of the Lord. Prophet Eli's sin was not disciplining his children for their sinful behavior.

In 1 Samuel 3:11-13, the Lord told Samuel: "See, I am about to do something in Israel that will make the ears of everyone who hears of it tingle. At that time I will carry out against Eli everything I spoke against his family—from beginning to end. For I told him that I would judge his family forever because of the sin he knew about; his sons made themselves contemptible and he failed to restrain them."

There is clarity in the Word of God concerning discipline: "He who spares his rod hates his son, but he who loves him disciplines him promptly" (Proverbs 13:24 NKJV). You see, lack of Eli's parental discipline made the children vile and eventually cost them their inheritance from the Lord. It is very important that we discipline our child while there is hope because there comes a time when such discipline becomes difficult or impossible because they are now set in their ways, and at such times it takes the grace of the Lord to wean them off their corrupt heart.

Yes, I know it's never too late for God and nothing is impossible for Him. Many of the problems we face today result from the failure of someone to take the required action at the appropriate time. It is, however, important to avoid shouting at, abusing, or cursing your child and using derogatory language like "stupid" or "fool." Neither should you modify behavior with indiscriminate flogging. Avoid losing your temper and using it as an excuse to beat up your child. If you do that, it only proves you are unable to control your temper and exhibits a bad example to your child.

Proverbs 20:7 states, "The righteous man walks in his integrity; his children are blessed after him." The lack of integrity on the part of the prophet Eli disqualified his lineage from the promised blessing and honor.

In 2 Samuel 18:29, David asked the question "Is the young man Absalom safe?" His question came too late because his son was already dead and buried in a pit (verse 17). David was a brave man and giant killer, but he lacked the courage to discipline his son Absalom, to the extent that Absalom became a cold-blooded killer who eventually wanted his father's crown and life (2 Samuel 15:14). It is important that we do not make the same mistake of waiting too late before disciplining our children in love.

A child who is rebelling against their parents' leadership is heading towards disaster. Deuteronomy 5:16 states, "Honor your father and your mother, as the LORD your God has commanded you, that your days may be long, and that it may be well with you in the land which the LORD your God is giving you." Absalom failed to honor his father and was eventually taught a hard lesson, leading to his death.

The fact is that very few people fear God today. If they did, the murder rate would drop to an insignificant level. Rape, incest, and child abuse would be almost nonexistent because the reverence, respect, love, and desire to obey His command would prevent the offender from doing their evil deeds and wrongs to society. As a parent myself, I totally sympathize with every parent struggling to maintain a good moral discipline for their child. I have the upmost respect for single parents trying their best to bring up a child single-handedly or working parents coming home often tired and exhausted and having to deal with rude behavior at home and finding themselves lashing out at the child.

I am aware the pull of the world and its immoral view appears to be stronger in a long, drawn-out battle for supremacy. Every home is fighting this battle, the schools and colleges are fighting the same battle, and so is society at large. For believers, I have the assurance that the battle is of the Lord, and He has never lost any battle. He is full of patience and very merciful. Walking according to His commands may not seem fashionable, but it is the only way out of this problem. It is important that we discipline our children so as to enjoy a peaceful future. Purpose to win the battle today, refuse to be intimidated by teenagers' strategy of intimidation, be persistent and consistent, and our future should be peaceful. Resolve to remove the problem from the embryo (initial) stage, and by so doing you'll remove a socially polluting disease from our society.

In his message "Into the Storm," Steve Troxel of God's Daily Word Ministries says,

> God sometimes sends us into difficult situations to get our attention and draw us closer to Himself. These storms may be used to teach us basic truths or gently nudge us

back onto His path. But the storms may also be used to make major corrections in our course or adjustments in our character. Each is a form of discipline. Each is given with His perfect love. And each should be viewed as a wonderful opportunity for growth.

I absolutely share brother Troxel's view and believe we should not run away from the problem, but embrace it and learn from the situation. Learning is the greatest way of behaving better.

The book of Hebrews chapter 12 verse 6-7 states, "The Lord disciplines those He loves, and He punishes everyone He accepts as a son. Endure hardship as discipline; God is treating you as sons. For what son is not disciplined by his father?" Our heavenly Father loves us simply because we are His children, not because of what we do or accomplish. He desires nothing more than for his children to say, "I love You, Daddy!" But He also loves us enough to shape and mold us until we are "conformed to the likeness of His Son" (Romans 8:29).

None of us have yet been perfected; we are still being perfected through the work of the Holy Spirit. We are all flawed vessels with many rough edges—being conformed to the image of Jesus—and the process of smoothing out our rough edges can be quite uncomfortable. "No discipline seems pleasant at the time, but painful. Later on, however, it produces a harvest of righteousness and peace for those who have been trained by it" (Hebrews 12:11).

His hands of discipline are always purposeful and precise, and administered with great love. They are never out of control like so many angry hands in the world. His hands welcomed us into His kingdom by grace and are now ready to guide us on a wonderful journey. Our values and goals will begin to change as we draw closer to God and keep our eyes focused on Jesus. But along the way, as our rough edges are continually smoothed, we must learn a joyful submission to His loving hands of discipline.

BEING A GOOD CHRISTIAN PARENT

In this ever-increasing age of worldly TV programs and secular humanist education, what is a Christian parent to do in order to maintain intimacy with Christ and family?

Parents need to actively practice a combination of the suggestions below:

Read the Bible with them, pray with them, hug them, listen to them, love them, and share with them. Teach them, go places together, play with them, enjoy being with them, guide them, encourage them. Never lie to them. Be sincere with your children, teach them right from wrong, and share the love of Jesus with them.

Tell them about Jesus. Show them the love of Jesus. Teach them to pray to their heavenly Father in the mighty name of Jesus. Teach them about sin and how it displeases the Lord. Tell them about God's forgiveness. Teach them to forgive. Tell them your testimony and how Jesus saved you from your sins. Tell them about what God has done for you. Tell them how Jesus loves them so very much and how He died for them and rose again.

Plant Bible verses within their hearts every day of their life without being pushy. Teach them about God's forgiveness. Instill biblical values. Pray with them. Pray for their friends and teachers. Pray for the bullies at school. Discuss at dinner how their day went at school. Listen to their stories. Help them with their homework. Be friendly with them.

Notice them. Acknowledge them. Be attentive to their problems and struggles. If they are pulling away from you and are quiet about their problems, seek them out. Children desire attention and want to feel that they are appreciated and loved. They want to be noticed.

Look in their eyes when you talk with them. Listen to them. Be a good listener. Forget your worries for the moment and concentrate only on them. Notice when they're acting differently.

Laugh at their jokes. Relate to them. If you cannot relate to them, ask the Lord to teach you how to relate to them so you can be "cool" in their book. Respect them and treasure them. They are your gift from the Lord. They are little people with feelings and dreams.

Be flexible when needed. Be excited when you see them. Tell them how special they are in God's eyes. Let them make mistakes. Help them to learn from those mistakes. Ask them what they have learned. Invest your time in them.

Teach them to be responsible. Give them tasks or chores to do around the house. Teach them accountability. They must stand accountable for their own actions. Include them in decision-making. Ask for their opinions. Welcome their suggestions. If you are buying a house, take them along. Include them in the process so they will better understand how things work in the real world. If you have a business, take them to work and let them learn to appreciate what you do and what it takes to make money that is provided for them.

Notice when they grow. Help them mature into fine adults by giving them good biblical instruction. You can better prepare them for life by teaching them godly principles, and then the more comfortable they will be out in the real world.

Teach them manners. Tell them why manners are important. Include them in conversations. This is very important because children develop their social skills by interacting at home.

Instil truth of the Word of God in them. Believe what they say. Be rational and never shout at them for telling the truth. Be understanding. You have to remember; they are being very brave in telling you the awful truth and keep this in mind. Encourage them to tell you the truth in the future by not yelling and screaming at them. If you do, they will begin to lie to you to avoid punishment. Instead, pray for understanding. Tell them you appreciate them for admitting the truth. Tell them you are displeased with what they have done but are very pleased in the fact that they told you the truth. Make sure you let them know that your love for them is unconditional. This they will feel from you by your words but especially by your actions. Love them no matter what. Consistency is the key.

> All scripture is given by inspiration of God, and is profitable for doctrine, for reproof, for correction, for instruction in righteousness.   (2 Timothy 3:16, KJV)

Ask the Lord to help you to be the best godly parent that you can be. The Lord can enable you to teach your children His ways. He will lead them into His paths.

When we put the above into practice, we are not only enforcing intimacy with God but also with ourselves and the family at large.

THE FINAL WORD

I heard a story where a father and son were climbing a dangerous mountain. The father said, "Son, be very careful. We are coming to a very dangerous place." The boy replied, "Daddy, don't worry, I'm putting my feet where you put yours." Parents, that's exactly what our children are doing. They are watching what we do and where we go. They are listening to what we say and checking to see if it aligns with our actions.

David failed as the father of Absalom, but tragedy and heartache followed the entire family of David (2 Samuel 13:7-39). David failed partly because he was a prodigal father, and never home to bring God's perspective into the upbringing of his children, and his children followed in his footsteps, mimicking his poor example of parenting. By his sin with Bathsheba and the murder of Uriah (2 Samuel 11), David broke one of the Lord's commands regarding murder and his children followed him. David repented of his sin, but Absalom refused to repent, a factor that led to his eventual death.

I would like to leave you with the following principles. Adhering to them should serve our families well as we face the challenges of life.

1. Rule your house well, having children that submit to your leadership with all reverence (1 Timothy 3:4).

2. Ensure that your child walks with the wise and decent people for a companion of fools will be destroyed (Proverbs 13:20).

3. Do not allow outside influences to destroy your good child upbringing principles because "evil company corrupts good habits" (1 Corinthians 15:33).

4. Vet and protect the relationship of your sons and daughters to ensure they are "not unequally yoked together with unbelievers" (2 Corinthians 6:14). Dating a questionable

character may corrupt your child or create emotional attachment to the wrong type of people.

5. Rescuing your child from a corrupt relationship is saving a life, especially a life entrusted into your care to bring up in the ways of the Lord. As you would not be shy to drag your child out of a burning building, likewise, you should not be shy about dragging your child out of a corrupt relationship.

6. Be firm and avoid child intimidation or wearing-out strategy. Rule your house well, but be fair and consistent.

7. Be a good role model because your child watches all your moves and copies them. Parents who are always swearing and cursing should not be surprised if their children start to do the same because children tend to imitate their parents' good and bad habits.

8. Invest in your child by giving them time and teaching them the wisdom God had poured into your heart and allow them to reap the positive benefits of your life experience. Walk with the Spirit of God and express the love, peace, and joy found in our heavenly Father to your child.

9. Do not overindulge your child. As God prospers the work of your hand and wealth becomes your "friend" and "companion," your ability to afford luxurious but nonessential items is increased. Overindulging your child with such luxury without proper training in respecting and appreciating these items may lead to their destruction.

In 2 Samuel 15:1, the Bible tells us that Absalom provided himself with chariots and horses, and fifty men to run before him. David was a great warrior and a very principled person (except regarding women); however, he overindulged his children. They didn't have to work and so became playboys who were concerned about fun, their inheritance, and not what they could work for by their sweat. They were corrupted by abundance, overindulgence, and a lack of discipline in their family. The failures led to Absalom wanting to usurp his father's throne and his eventual untimely death.

Beloved, discipline in love should not be taken as a license for physical, verbal, or emotional abuse of your children. It should be a love action done today in order to ensure a better tomorrow. If you really love your child, please coach, educate, guide, instruct, teach, counsel, train, help, and prune the rough edges because all these love actions will prepare them for a more rewarding adult life.

PRAYER

Father, teach me to love even when things go wrong, and to be patient and kind when the children are underfoot. Help me to overlook the spiteful words of an angry spouse, and to rejoice when someone at the office gets the raise I thought I needed. Teach me to talk in love, to lay gossip quietly aside, and to take up words of grace instead.

The Intimacy of Love

Love never fails. According to Dr Segun Oshinaga[8], "Lust deforms but love reforms." Nothing works without it, and there can be no failure with it. When you live by love, you cannot fail. It takes faith to believe that love's way will not fail. The natural mind cannot understand that because as humans we are ruled by selfishness. But when you practice love by faith and refuse to seek your own, you put the Father into action on your behalf. As long as you stay in love, God the Father seeks your own. He sees to it that you succeed. Walking in love is to your great advantage.

> Love bears up under anything and everything that comes, and is ever ready to believe the best of every person, its hopes are fadeless under all circumstances and it endures everything [without weakening]. Love never fails—never fades out or becomes obsolete or comes to an end.
>
> (1 Corinthians 13:7-8, AMP)

Agape love is a new kind of power. It makes you master of every situation. In Isaiah 54:17, the Lord says that "no weapon formed against you will prosper" (NKJV). No one even has the

---

8   Dr. Segun Oshinuga—a casual discussion speech 2017.

power to hurt your feelings because you are not ruled by feelings but by God's love.

This love is revolutionary. If we fully understood the great return from living God's love, we would probably be competing with each other, each of us trying to love the other more. And without a doubt, everyone would emerge from that competition a winner. For love is truly the only sure secret to our success.

RECIPE FOR A HAPPY CHRISTIAN MARRIAGE

Make sure you put Jesus first and then all things will be added.

Each and every day use the following ingredients:

- 1 gallon of prayer and the reading of God's Word while praising God for His many blessings.
- 2 cups of encouragement, kindness, and gentleness while both maintaining a regular loving communication
- 1 cup of consideration, courtesy, and thoughtfulness
- 1 cup of contentment and understanding of one another's faults
- 1 cup of understanding of each other's needs seasoned with cooperation
- 3 teaspoons pure extract of "I'm sorry" when needed

Add all the things you like to do together (hobbies), sweeten well with plentiful love and affection. Always stir well with the Golden Rule.

The Lord Jesus said in Luke 6:31: "And as ye would that men should do to you, do ye also to them likewise" (KJV). Imagine reciprocating the above recipe. Your level of intimacy will surely increase tremendously and love will surely reign within that relationship. I would also like readers to consider the Scriptures below with regards to the intimacy of love in our life.

> That Christ may dwell in your hearts by faith; that ye, being rooted and grounded in love, may be able to comprehend with all saints what is the breadth, and length, and depth, and height; And to know the love of Christ, which passeth knowledge, that ye might be filled with all the fullness of God.   (Ephesians 3:17-19, KJV)

We have a double metaphor in the verses above, both taken from agriculture. As trees, we are to be rooted in love; therein our souls are to grow into the infinite love of God, and from this love we derive all the nourishment that is essential for our full growth till we fully have the same mind that was in Jesus Christ. When we achieve this, the above ingredients will be present and working in us to the glory of God our Father.

> And whatsoever ye do in word or deed, do all in the name of the Lord Jesus, giving thanks to God and the Father by him.   (Colossians 3:17, KJV)

This verse in Colossians sounds like a command to do everything with integrity and a desire to honor the Lord, and His glory should be our aim. Our relationships, especially marriage, would blossom and be filled with greater love if our focus and the ultimate goal were to honor Christ and bring glory to Him. Thanksgiving will continually flow from our heart and we would engage in every duty, not only in the name of Christ, but with thankfulness for strength and the privilege to know Him better.

> Wives, submit yourselves unto your own husbands, as it
> is fit in the Lord. Husbands, love your wives, and be not
> bitter against them.   (Colossians 3:18-19, KJV)

The next two verses in Colossians describe the pressing duties of the Christian life, and they unfortunately have become a bone of contention in the modern household because everyone is jostling for power within the marriage. If our marriage is to glorify the Lord, we must never separate the privileges and duties of the gospel as intended by our Lord Jesus. Submission is the duty of the wives giving honor to the husband, but not to be used as a servant, and certainly not submission to a severe lord or stern tyrant, but to her own husband, who is engaged to affectionate duty. According to the practices of the holy principles, the husband is intended to be the leader in the marriage union. And husbands must love their wives with tender and faithful affection. They must be both just and diligent without selfish designs or hypocrisy and disguise.

It's important to note that the duty of husband to "love" is more stringent than that of submission, because to love is to sacrifice everything, just as Christ sacrificed Himself for us on the cross. It's not a duty to die as Jesus already died for us, but it requires sacrificial love because when you love your wife, you are loving yourself. Since the woman was made out of the man, out of his rib (Genesis 2:21-24), she must not be trampled under his feet, but stay by his side, a "help meet" to him at all times (Genesis 2:18).

> And whatsoever ye do, do it heartily, as to the Lord,
> and not unto men; Knowing that of the Lord ye shall
> receive the reward of the inheritance: for ye serve the
> Lord Christ.   (Colossians 3:23-24, KJV)

This is speaking to all of us, the husband and the wife and all the well-wishers. Whatever you do for your wife or husband, do it heartily, not by mere force and necessity, grudgingly, and with murmurings, but from the heart, and with goodwill, having a true, real, and hearty affection for each other, having their interest at heart. And delight in serving each other, like the Hebrew servant who loved his master, and the wife or husband who won't depart from one another. Furthermore, do these things without expecting or demanding your reward from your partner, but be assured that your ultimate reward comes from the Lord, who never forgets our acts of love.

Beloved, whatever you do, allow God to be in the center of your relationships, and ensure it is filled with intimacy, which encompasses feelings of attachment, closeness, and bondedness. In addition, let passion and sexual attraction drive you on—and commitment keep you attached to one another. Without these ingredients, love would struggle to survive. Patience, forgiveness, and mutual understanding of each other's faults go a long way to ensure your success where others are failing. We must always be each other's keeper.

GOD HAS FEELINGS FOR YOU

> And hope does not put us to shame, because God's love has been poured out into our hearts through the Holy Spirit, who has been given to us.   (Romans 5:5, NIV)

It takes a loving person to pour out himself to others. Likewise, it takes a loving and intimate God, despite our weaknesses and rebellion, to pour out His love into our hearts through the Holy Spirit, and we are forever grateful. In 1 John 4:19 we are told that we loved Him because He first loved us. If we know beyond any shadow of doubt that God loves us, I do not believe we would ever be depressed. Sadly, many of us (Christians included) are not fully persuaded about this love because of the circumstances around us. We need to fully trust Him to take care of these problems without allowing Satan to deposit or activate fear and anxiety in our spirit that could lead to physical, emotional, and spiritual problems.

Intellectual knowledge of God's love is not enough; our whole being (spirit, soul, and body) must be convinced of His love. We cannot, however, achieve this by our own power, so it is the Holy Spirit who can give us this assurance. Then, we become fully persuaded just like David in Psalm 23:4: "Even though I walk through the valley of the shadow of death, I will fear no evil, for you are with me; your rod and staff, they comfort me." David had intimacy with the Lord in spite of his challenges. We also need to know the Lord intimately. And when those situations threaten to overwhelm us, we know and are fully assured of His love to save, protect, and guide us.

The apostle Paul expresses a prayer that grows out of his awareness of all that God is doing in the life of believers (Ephesians 3:16-20). He knew that God's love for us is so great that it cannot be completely known. The truth is, we can know this love as a reality in our lives through an intimate relationship with Jesus Christ. In Ephesians 4:1-16, Paul also encourages us to love and forgive one another, starting with the church, as we must live by example to live and work together in unity, and grow together in maturity.

I believe it's absolutely impossible to have Jesus in our lives and not feel His presence. He wants us to fully experience His love, for only then can we totally respond to Him. People who have never experienced God's love in this way can only offer

Him an intellectual love in return. I believe strongly that it is the lack of a deep and total love relationship with God that leaves people wide open to insecurity, fear, and anxiety. Now let's go deeper with God to know the length, breadth, depth, and width of His love.

WHAT DO WE DO WITH GOD'S LOVE?

First, we must express God's love to others. In Romans 5:5, the Bible tells us that God shed His love abroad in our hearts by the Holy Spirit, so we not only need to tell people about God's love; we also need to show them the love of Christ by our actions that flow from us to others so that they can do likewise to other people, because this is how we multiply God's love on planet earth.

Second, we need to learn to trust one another. In this current age, there is little trust for one another and people do not trust themselves. It is important to know that love doesn't exist in weariness and mistrust as this affects our relationship with one another. Our love does not depend on doing everything right. It is, in fact, when we make mistakes that the love of others is most needed, and most expressed. It is comforting to know that if I make a mistake, I will not be rejected by family, team members, friends, and pastors, but will receive the correction I need at that moment out of the love we have for each other.

The Bible says, "If a brother or sister is naked, and destitute of daily food, and one of you says to them, 'Depart in peace, be warmed and filled,' but you do not give them the things that are needed for the body, what does it profit?" (James 2:15-16 NKJV). The apostle James is simply telling us: it is not enough to tell people that you love them, there must be an outward demonstration that you do. A lack of love can lead to loneliness, rejection, insecurity, fear, resentment, and eventually depression. On the other hand, the fullness of God's love brings security, peace, joy, and hope for a bright future in Him.

In Matthew 14:30, the apostle Peter gives us a tremendous example of how to react: when he began to sink, he did not wait until he was totally immersed in the water; rather, he immediately cried out to the Lord for help. I believe we should follow Peter's example and cry to the Lord when we face that sinking feeling—not trust in our own strength because it will fail us. Contrary to popular teaching, I believe the Lord did not rebuke Peter. He just offered help and got him out of the jam. He walked him back into the boat victorious through the eyes of love, and showed him the grace of God.

That's how to live in victory after failure. Peter had begun to fail by sinking. He called to Jesus for help, and yet he walked on the water again. He victoriously walked back to the boat with Jesus. Through His heart of love, Jesus takes our failures and turns them into stepping-stones for success. If you feel like crying out to Jesus, stop whatever you're doing right now and go ahead; don't let the feelings of failure escalate into depression by waiting to call out to Him. Do it now because Jesus loves you intimately and wants to lift you up and out of every mess.

PRAYER

Jesus, increase the ability of Your children to love, so that we may be witnesses in a world without love. By Your grace, make Your love in us increase and overflow for each other and for everyone else, just as ours does for You (1 Thessalonian 3:12). *Amen.*

Give Me an Attitude of Gratitude

Attitude is intangible and can't be tasted or smelled. However, most people instinctively know the difference between a good and bad attitude. You tend to recognize attitudes by what people say or do (or both). In the Bible, Jesus taught us about an attitude of gratitude using the story of the ten lepers who were healed, and only one of them (a Samaritan) returned to give thanks (Luke 17:12-19). There is a tremendous potential in giving thanks as it releases the miracle-working power of God and seals the blessing received.

Jesus said, "Rise and go; your faith has made you well" (verse 19). Nine were healed in an exclusively physical sense, and the tenth, who came back to give thanks to God, was healed not only physically but also spiritually. He was brought into a right, eternal relationship with God. The nine received a partial, temporary blessing while the tenth received a total, permanent blessing. The difference was his attitude of gratitude.

In order to understand this important virtue properly, I believe it is a godly idea to define our terms. What is attitude? It's "the way a person thinks and behaves."⁹ That is one's approach to life, disposition (tendency or habit), and frame of mind. It includes one's opinion, outlook, stance, manner, perspective and point of view. Gratitude is a feeling of being grateful for gifts or favors. It is appreciation, indebtedness, obligation, recognition, and thankfulness.

WHAT ARE WE GRATEFUL FOR?

In today's world of immediate gratification, people forget to say thank you for what they have received from the Lord. We are grateful for the blessings endowed upon us. Ephesians 1:3 says, "Blessed be the God and Father of our Lord Jesus Christ, who has blessed us with every spiritual blessing in the heavenly places in Christ." Allow me to share some of these blessings below so that we may recall them when needed, and through the process of reflection, deep gratitude may flow from our hearts:

1. We are blessed in Christ Jesus (Ephesians 1:1-3).

2. We are chosen in Him and adopted by Christ (verses 4-5).

3. We are accepted in the beloved (verses 5-6).

4. We are redeemed and forgiven in Christ (verse 7).

5. We have our inheritance in Christ (verses 12-13).

6. Our faith is built in Christ (verse 15).

7. Our wisdom and hope is found in Christ (verses 17-18).

8. Our hope is in Christ (verse 18).

9. We have power in Christ (verses 19-20).

---

9   *Collins Concise Dictionary & Thesaurus*, 3rd ed. (2003).

FATHER, TEACH ME HOW TO LOVE AGAIN

10. We overcome in Christ (verses 21-22).

11. We are partakers of His promise in Christ (Ephesians 3:6).

12. We have boldness and access to the Father through Christ (verse 12).

When we examine carefully and fully understand the above provisions for all believers, our hearts should be full of gratitude, knowing full well that our calling and position have been planned and executed by God the Father, the Son, and the Holy Spirit before the foundation of the world (Ephesians 1:4). When we all know our calling and provision in Christ, our hearts will flow with the utmost joy for the One who in ages past had been thinking about us, loving us, and planning to bless us, irrespective of Satan's failed attempts to sabotage us.

We receive the spirit of joy amid trouble and problems because the joy of the Lord is our strength (Nehemiah 8:10). Paul called the Church to have Christian unity and joy in Philippians 3:1 and 4:4. Paul is the rejoicing apostle, and he urges us to do the same regardless of our circumstances, as joy drives out discord and enables our hearts to be full of gratitude in the midst of trials.

THREE TYPES OF ATTITUDE

AN ATTITUDE OF JOY

Joy is an attitude that flows from the heart, the very place where gratitude flows from. Although in prison, Paul had cultivated an attitude of prayer so much that he could find the strength to pray for his friends. He said in Philippians 1:3-4, "I thank my God every time I remember you. In all my prayers for all of you, I always pray with joy." That's an attitude of gratitude and selflessness fully cultivated and manifesting itself at all times. He was grateful to God for saving him, and he did not allow his present circumstances to cloud his judgment; instead, he chose to intercede for others.

It is important to know that, for those of us who are saved, someone had been praying for us before we finally accepted Christ as Lord and Savior. It is equally our duty to pray others into the kingdom of God. In doing so, we are showing our appreciation to God for saving us from eternal judgment. Why not talk to God right now about your friends, neighbors, and family members without Christ and do it with joy, passion, and gratitude? Why not make your number one aim and purpose to glorify Him?

Paul showed his love and trust in God in Philippians 1:21 by declaring, "For me to live is Christ"—an attitude of gratitude. In today's fast-paced world, gratitude seems to be quickly disappearing. Instead of saying like Paul, "For to me to live is Christ," they say

- "For me to live is wealth," declared the businessman.
- "For me to live is knowledge," declared the scholar.
- "For me to live is victory," declared the soldier.
- "For me to live is pleasure," declared the young man.
- "For me to live is fame," declared the *X-Factor* and reality show contestant—and some Christian ministers.

All of the above people do not know or fail to understand that Christ is the giver of life. He says, "I am come that you might have life" (John 10:10)—a selfless attitude of a Savior. James 1:17 puts it like this: "Every good thing and every perfect gift is from above, coming down from the Father of lights, with whom there is no variation or shifting shadow" (NASB).

We need to recognize that our gifts come from God, and we should be thankful for them and stop boasting. If we receive a gift from a friend or family member, we are normally grateful and say thank you. It is important that we do the same for our heavenly Father, who has given everything, and say thank you. Psalm 100:4 admonishes us to "enter his gates with thanksgiving and his courts with praise." It simply means to show gratitude with joy in our heart and praise in our mouth.

Being thankful and full of gratitude is a state of mind, and we have to constantly work on our thoughts so as to remain positive in the midst of testing circumstances. We have to train ourselves to feel thankful and see the good in our lives on a regular basis. Gratitude turns denial into acceptance; chaos into order; darkness into light; and creates a vision for tomorrow that turns failure into a magnificent success. We need to be grateful for both known and unknown blessings so that we not only see them but possess them.

AN ATTITUDE OF LOVE

In the first half of Philippians chapter 2, the apostle Paul tells us we have the mind of Christ that is filled with joy, harmony, and divine appreciation of one another. When we adopt the attitude of gratitude, we do nothing through strife, selfishness, and arrogance; instead, we have regard for the other person and think highly of one another. The attitude of love and mutual respect endears us to be grateful to our friends and the people God has put in our lives. We must learn to esteem the good in others above that which is in ourselves, and by so doing we exhibit the mind of Christ in Philippians 2:5. The apostle Paul tells us to be humble as Christ was humble, and allow God to exalt us as he was highly exalted and rewarded for his humiliation. Why not ask the Holy Spirit to assist you in cultivating this attitude of gratitude?

A NEGATIVE ATTITUDE

As much of our behavior depends on our attitude, whether positive or negative, we generate happiness or unhappiness; we can be filled with joy or a host of psychological and physiological disorders. Hence, we need to exercise control over our thoughts in order to achieve good health and increased personal effectiveness in every area of our lives. Therefore, if we are negative in life, there is a tendency to draw negativity towards ourselves, thereby invoking a dark cloud over our lives that in turn separate us from the highest good. On the other hand, if we are constantly positive even during various challenges, seeing the good in everything and everyone, there is blue sky and sunshine all around us and within us. In short, we are encouraged to fill our lives with love, faith, hope, and godly fulfilment, and all these help us maintain positive thoughts, which leads to a positive attitude.

In Deuteronomy 5:22-32, the children of Israel did not show gratitude to the Lord after delivering them from the bondage of servitude in Egypt. Instead of gratitude they murmured and complained because of the challenges faced en route to the promised land. The Lord fed them with manna and none of them got sick or wanted for anything. He led them with a pillar of fire by night and a cloud by day until they came to Mount Sinai. However, they still found a reason to complain despite hearing the voice of the Lord. They simply did not have the attitude of gratitude.

HOW DOES A NEGATIVE ATTITUDE AFFECT OUR RELATIONSHIP WITH GOD?

ADAM AND EVE

In Genesis 3:8-10, after eating the forbidden fruit, Adam and Eve heard the Lord God walking in the garden to have fellowship with the first couple of creation. They became afraid and hid themselves, thus breaking the time of fellowship with Him. Likewise, sin usually releases a negative attitude that drives us away from God and interrupts our time of fellowship in prayer and the study of His Word. Negative attitudes tend to rob us of God's purpose and blessings.

OFFERING TIME

The Bible highlights the influence of our attitudes on our relationship with God (Genesis 4:1-16). Here, we read the story of the Adam's children (Cain and Abel). It was the time to bring an offering to the Lord with an upright heart and with such sacrifices pleasing to Him to honor Him in appreciation according to the level He had prospered them. I believe that God had communicated the requirement of these offerings, including the time and location.

Cain brought an offering of the fruit of the ground to the Lord, and Abel also brought of the firstborn of his flock and their fat. The Bible tells us that the Lord respected Abel and his offering but did not respect Cain and his offering. However, the Bible does not say why God fail to respect (or reject) Cain's offering, but we are told that Cain became angry and his countenance fell. In other words, he began to exhibit a negative attitude. Perhaps Cain did not do the will of God by acting with the wrong attitude and motives. He had a "form of godliness" but denied its power (2 Timothy 3:5).

In comparison, Abel's offering was an act of saving faith (Ephesians 2:8-9). "By faith Abel offered to God a more excellent sacrifice than Cain, through which he obtained witness from God that he was righteous" (Hebrews 11:4). By faith God declared him righteous.

As children of God, it is important to regularly check our motives so we don't act like hypocrites who hear many sermons, say many prayers, give money, and yet want for sincerity, and so come short of God's acceptance.

DAVID'S ATTITUDE

The Bible tells us about a boy who was neglected, rejected, and relegated to the bush by his family and tasked with looking after the sheep. In the wilderness, he contemplated the wonders of creation and learned to love the heavenly Father. His heart began to overflow with extravagant worship for his Father in heaven, and God was pleased with him and called him "a man after my own heart" (Acts 13:22). The man in question is David; he did not allow circumstances to kill his relationship with the Father of all fathers.

David was grateful for life in the wilderness as he was his own boss and the wilderness was a place of preparation for greatness. He was being groomed as a great warrior who eventually killed Goliath and became king of Israel. We need to develop this attitude of gratitude daily through relationship and worship while giving thanks to God for giving us victory, health, strength, and provision every day. *Thank you, Jesus! Lord, teach me the attitude of gratitude on a daily basis. Amen.*

WHAT GRATITUDE
CAN DO FOR HUMANKIND

Gratitude enables us to focus on good things that happen to us rather than the bad. Our ability to adopt this way of thinking and behavioral pattern ensures amongst other things that depression is averted. An attitude of gratitude lifts us above the tides of life when we start to thank God for every situation and circumstance. It is also important that we take these things to God in prayer and use our experience as a source of strength so that the God of peace (Jehovah Shalom) can help us.

Gratitude helps us to remove self-centeredness and realize the place where God has placed us. We then begin to recognize that the battle belongs to the Lord and we are part of something bigger than ourselves. Our love for the Lord is awakened as we are constantly grateful for His gifts and favor—we are protected from the fiery darts of the enemy, and our hearts respond with thanksgiving while God pours out His love on us.

CULTIVATING AN
ATTITUDE OF GRATITUDE

Ephesians 5:20 encourages us to give thanks always for all things. It means that we ought to give thanks, not for some things, but *for all things*. Paul was in prison when he wrote the letter to the Ephesians, yet he was rejoicing in the Lord. He gratefully turned his prison into a palace; however, ungratefulness can easily turn a palace into prison.

It is important that we cultivate a daily attitude of gratitude and not occasionally when we see something special done in our lives. Being in the land of the living and having food on the table and clothes to wear is worth thanking the Lord for. Why?

Because other people would like to be in your position but just cannot be.

We need to write down those things we are grateful for and acknowledge the goodness of the Lord in our lives and families. It is important to appreciate our parents (both spiritual and biological), our friends, our family members, our brothers and sisters in Christ, our church, and the shepherd placed over us, letting these attitudes become infectious and widely noticeable. We must make merry music in our heart to God and make it a way of life so much that our heart appreciates the Lord in our sleep. Our inner joy eliminates worry, trouble, and daily stress.

Our gratitude should be genuine if we truly believe that every good thing comes from the Lord, and not achieved by luck, hard work, or wisdom. Likewise, our gratitude must be permanent and long-term and not just one day a year, for God daily loads us with benefits. Every prayer should also be sealed with thanks, believing that we already have the answers. Likewise, our gratitude is to be infectious and widely noticeable.

PRAYER

Thank you, Lord, for the simple daily things in life. For not being fired for mistakes at work. For my family and my health, for food and shelter. And for sorrowful things like heartache, pain, and suffering, for I know it is You, God, who works all things together for my good (Romans 8:28).

LOVE EIGHT

Teach Me to Love Again

The main purpose of this chapter is to encourage you by sharing some of the testimonies of people for whom God has restored broken relationships and taught the ways of love. If we draw an analogy from the work of car mechanics, they repair—restore— renew. This process makes me wonder how often we ought to take our heart for repairs before the Lord and what our expectation is. We constantly maintain our cars by checking and replacing the brakes, changing and checking the fluids (engine oil, brake fluid, gear oil), air in the tires, belts, etc. I wonder how diligent we are with our needed heart maintenance with God, the Master mechanic.

Are we carefully and constantly maintaining our relationship with Him? For something to last it takes perseverance and maintenance over time (that is a good picture of the Lord). In order to maintain our deep relationship with the Lord, we have to pay attention to Him. That requires regular face time with Him, that is in His Word and in prayer. Our time with Him cannot be an afterthought. If that happens, then we will break down and be vulnerable to Satan's attack.

Let us go to the place where repair starts and He will teach us how to love again. He will give us rest. Isaiah 58:11 says, "The Lord will guide you continually, and satisfy your soul in drought, and strengthen your bones; you shall be like a watered garden, and like a spring of water, whose waters do not fail." We just need to go back to the greatest love and say, "Father, teach me how to love again." He will repair, restore, and renew.

The lyrics of David Charvet's song "Teach Me How to Love" convey my sentiment in this area. David says, "I don't wanna slip nor trip again as I'm falling in love again. I want to get it right for it's the time of my life; it's time of picking up the pieces that I know I left behind. I can feel it coming back again and so I've got to give it one more try as giving up is not my style."

In the midst of this, David confesses that he needed to be taught how to love again.

Like David, most of us need to be real with our Lord and say, "I really don't know anything about walking in your love again; I need to refill and restore my broken relationship with you, Lord. Please teach me how to love again so as to become a true reflection of my Father in heaven."

As an encouragement, I would like to you readers some testimonies of people who have previously been outcasts in the realm of love, only to rediscover the Father's love again. They were mainly from Restore Ministries, but some were personal interviews; however, their true identities have been concealed.

> And they overcame him because of the blood of the Lamb and because of the word of their testimony, and they did not love their life even to death.   (Revelation 12:11)

ONE—RESTORED FROM CRIMINALITY[10]

In his own words, M. L. was born into an English traveller family and lived amongst a family of criminals. He lived his life as he liked, did steroids, learned to fight, and watched his brother fight. He was led to Christ at the tender age of thirteen by a Christian minister Ron Sims during a visit to his boarding school. He spent most of his life as a force of destruction for over 25 years being manipulated by the dark forces that wreak havoc in the world. Most of his life he was in and out of prison. He spent at least six out of the past ten years locked up in jail. At other times, he lived like a don, wasting his ill-gotten money on loose living and on the run in Spain and Europe. He had been arrested about five hundred times since childhood, and had used at least twenty aliases.

M. L. was constantly chasing the "dream" (money, drugs, women, guns, cars, houses) as he believed something was missing in his life. He became the top man in an organized criminal empire, making and wasting hundreds of thousands of British pounds on champagne and cars. He thought this was the way to live, and corrupted his children to think money was all they needed to be happy. However, he later realized that it was love, guidance, friendship, and a father figure that he really wanted. Then crime caught up with him and he became a fugitive again.

On the run in Spain for the second time, something went wrong and he got himself and his partner locked up but got out after three days. For a man who trusted in no one except number one (himself), a man who loved guns and mocking the police and the prison system, he could no longer find joy in these criminal

---

10 Transcript of interview with M. L.

activities. M. L. lay on the sofa depressed in an apartment in Spain, and the thought of Jesus, who he had received as Lord and Savior at the tender age of thirteen, filled his heart.

He started to call upon the Lord, and then began scanning through God TV. He studied the Bible and prayed night after night, looking for answers to many questions. After much struggle, M. L. finally heard the voice of God clearly directing him to put a stop to his fugitive life, and return to England in order to face the law and submit to authority.

However, stubbornness, hate, and distrust for the authorities were too great in his mind; he found it difficult to totally obey. After much showboating in court, firing three barristers [lawyers], and attempting to pervert the cause of justice, he eventually surrendered to God's will. He later secured a temporary release and threw himself totally without any inhibition to fellowship in church, seeking to be used especially for his testimony. However, he suffered a few knock-backs trying to fit into the structured Christian life.

He also had some success with believers rallying around him, providing help, mentoring, teaching, and discipleship. These were really fulfilling for him and he can boldly declare that Jesus is all he needs. He was eventually sentenced to imprisonment, and this time dedicated his days and resources to mentor, help, and minister to other offenders in jail. In his words, "I found that Jesus is REAL! I couldn't keep it in and had to tell others what Jesus had done for me."

M. L. said that he felt sorry for all the bad things and offences committed, and really would like forgiveness from all the victims of his crimes. He had made peace with the Lord and received His forgiveness too.

Within six months of being out of jail, M. L. had set up five legitimate companies and believes God restored all the enemy had stolen from him during prodigal years, and now declares, "As for me and my house, we will serve the Lord—we are free and saved. Hallelujah! And Jesus can set you free too, as we are all his work in progress."

M. L. would like to totally dedicate his life to the Lord with more zeal than he had serving Satan. That's an example of a life transformed by our Lord Jesus Christ in my humble opinion and I pray this newfound love is real and permanent and that he would be used like Saul (Paul), in Jesus' name. Amen.

TWO—HOW AND WHY I FELL IN LOVE WITH JESUS[11]

It was not my intention to become a Christian and certainly not fallen-in-love with Jesus—but I did anyway!

I have also thought that Christians are boring people devoid of the realities of modern life. Clubbing is my church. I thought becoming a Christian would mean the loss of my ability to party, drink, and enjoy the good things of life.

WHY DID I BECOME A CHRISTIAN?

An Alpha course was recommended to me by a very loving and God-fearing couple. While I resisted the idea at first, I eventually attended one near to my workplace, mainly out of curiosity and to test the truthfulness of the Bible.

At the Alpha course, I was very argumentative and noncooperative. Internally, I knew God was knocking at the door

---

11 By Sugar Babe.

of my heart and feared that if I opened the door, something was going to happen that would transform my life forever. This is what actually happened at the Alpha weekend—my worst fears had finally come true. As soon as the Holy Spirit was invited into the room, it felt like He just bypassed my barrier and *whoosh* went straight into my heart.

For the first time in my life, I felt this warm, loving, unnatural feeling that all the sex, drugs, and partying in this world could not produce. He touched me where I had never been touched before—"my heart"—and it was all too real.

Falling in love with Jesus is just my natural response to His love for me. I now see Jesus as my Savior, deliverer, a passionate lover, a great warrior and excellent teacher.

The Alpha course enabled me to realize the need for Jesus in my life. The veil was lifted and I was rescued from a life of no hope.

HOW DID I FALL IN LOVE WITH JESUS?

After the baptism in the Holy Spirit, I was still carrying on life as usual, but this time I was sin conscious. There were gradual changes in my life, but a great battle ensued in my mind for weeks. The changes were only brought home to me one night at the club. Everything looked different. God had opened my eyes and freed me from the desire for male attention, getting drunk, and smoking. I had a nasty argument with my best friend as we no longer saw things from the same perspective. I left the club really upset and I thought it was time that I make the commitment to Jesus since I'd come to the end of the road and I did not see things with the worldly eyes again.

Arriving at home, I got hold of the only Bible in my house that was given to me by a former boyfriend. I opened the book of Ecclesiastes. I immediately realized that wisdom is meaningless; pleasures are meaningless and all my toils are meaningless if not rightly related to God. I knew immediately that God was speaking to me through His Word as it seemed to perfectly describe my past and present circumstances.

My heart is now prepared, ripe for harvest into the kingdom of God. As I did not know how to pray, I believe God directed me to a Christian book called *The Fear Factor* by Akeem Shomade, which had been given to me when I opened his business account. I used the salvation prayer at the back of the book to commit my life to Christ. I asked for the forgiveness of sins and for Jesus to come into my life. After saying the prayer, something beautiful happened to me: immediately all the battle stopped and instantly I was free of the torment I had been going through for weeks. I knew peace like never before. As the author of *The Fear Factor* directed, I told everyone (especially my mother) who would listen that I have given my life to Jesus Christ.

My life is now totally dedicated to loving Jesus. I now see the church as a great body of exciting and loving people whose passion is for Jesus. I am really happy in my church and I cannot help but tell people about the saving power of Jesus. I now have an overwhelming love for Jesus and His people. The best relationship of my life has been coming to know Jesus Christ as my Savior.

HOW WOULD YOU DESCRIBE YOUR LOVE FOR GOD?

There's a part of my heart that feels complete to finally love someone with all of my heart. All of it! None left out. I love Jesus with a deep love from the very core of my inner being, maybe this is what the Bible calls the soul. I love God from a place in my heart I didn't even know existed. It's a crazy type of love because just when I think I have reached the peak of my "love for God" limit, I feel satisfied with a knowing that I love Him and I begin to notice something else about Him—His character, His heart—and I love Him even more. It sounds like a cliché, but I actually do feel like I love God more and more each day. I love him for who He is, I love Him for Jesus. I love Jesus for what He did and secured for me on the cross. He is my Hero and I owe my life to Him. I love Him because I know He is mine, my God! I love Him in a way I have never loved before. It's crazy and challenging, but it's beautiful, it's exciting, and just absolutely fabulous. It's indescribable. It just feels so natural and right. I love Him.

THREE—R. C. SHARES HER HEART, HER HUMOR, AND HER JOURNEY

I started out in life with few advantages, aside from a loving, encouraging mother and a creative mind. I was a dreamer and a deep thinker but unfortunately lacked discipline and focus. This meant I left school with only a few qualifications.

All throughout my higher education studies I worked full-time and studied part-time because money and success became my primary goal and ambition. I thoroughly enjoyed the security and privileges money and success awarded me. I drifted from one sales job to another, staying no longer than one to two years in any role, as I vigorously climbed the corporate ladder. Equally, I desired to jump ship so often because I would inevitably become disenchanted with the company, job role, or career progression prospects, as deep within me was an uncultivated desire to be free to run my own company.

I worked in call centers, business-to-business roles, especially telesales [telemarketing], and then I was a recruitment consultant, then an account manager, then a branch manager, then a consultant, and so on. I earned lots and lots of money, purchased all the creature comforts my heart could desire, but internally I found I was still discontent and needed to be filled with something higher.

During this journey, I became a Christian, I got married, we did some travelling together, and then had two wonderful children. Life was having its twists and turns, seeing me heading for a divorce after ten years of marriage. After this painful decision, I relocated and had the enormous task of choosing what to do with my broken life. One thing I decided I had to do promptly was change my surname [last name], as I was no longer married and carrying my ex-husband's surname was no longer necessary. As it happens, when I went to complete the name change legalities, I decided to change both of my names to something completely new! Little did I know that this was only the beginning of a radical makeover in my entire life.

The pain from my marriage breakup and subsequent divorce was worse than I could have ever imagined. The insecurities that arose from losing my secure foundation of church, marriage, and family life left my self-confidence shattered and I was desperately struggling with the isolation from the familiar life I had known, with a gnawing internal heaviness stemming from a lack of self-belief. This was a very painful and lonely place for me. Nothing was the same again! At this junction in my life, the only constant in my life was God and me. And I had my two children who remained my only loyal fans with unfaltering love, which was like soothing medicine through the darkest days of my life.

I was broken emotionally and drained mentally. For days I could not get dressed or go outside. I had hit rock bottom and everything I had come to know as "my life" was gone and broken forever. I had to literally rebuild a "new life" from the ground up. Eventually, thank God, I did three important things to kick start my life: I kept on believing in God, I began doing yoga for nearly two hours on a daily basis, and I redirected my energy from self-pity, hopelessness, and self-condemnation to reading everything I could on how to build my self-esteem, self-confidence, assertiveness skills, communication skills, success habits, and anything else that pertained to personal development, leadership skills, and spiritual growth. Before long I secured a very well-paid job, which after 15 months I resigned from to travel extensively around the world (including three Caribbean cruises), fell in love with a great guy, and indulged in a whirlwind VIP lifestyle and celebrity-style social life! I was living my dream life ... and loving it! But there was still a vacuum yet to be filled.

Yet, despite this highly intoxicating lifestyle, my life was groundless, chaotic, and had swung way out of balance. After three years of this incredible, yet somewhat self-indulgent lifestyle, I decided to return to my hometown and restart my attendance at my local church—to reestablish my relationship with God. (Admittedly, this decision was initiated by a strong conviction from God to return to church or risk losing my anointing and His Divine favor.)

This decision to return to my local church was not as easy as it might sound, because the last time most of my old friends and church family saw me I was happily married. Admittedly, I had left this old life rather abruptly, so there were many questions, some hostilities, rejections, jealousies, condemnations, and plain old rudeness. But, now I was emotionally and spiritually stronger, and so, somehow I was not fazed by this rebuff. I pressed on and deepened my understanding of the Word of God and grew my focus on spiritual matters. As each month passed, I gained more biblical knowledge and spiritually grew from strength to strength. After a few years of consistent focus on connecting with myself and God, I finally had a secure foundation and an anchor for my soul that felt "RIGHT." At last I had learned self-discipline and had a fresh spiritual awakening through the power of God's transforming Word.

Against all the odds, I was promoted to teaching and leadership roles within my local church and found a good, steady job again. Even though I was on my own now looking after my children, I was really enjoying parenting and had embraced the single life as a committed Christian. I began to build my wealth foundation by developing a modest property portfolio. Eventually, I was financially stable enough to finally give up the 9-to-5 grind to run my property business venture full-time. How great is our God!

After my property business success, I soon began considering lots more business ideas, but the one that I chose to follow up on was the Coaching and Training Consultancy as I was passionate about helping and being of assistance to others in "transition." Why? Because it was the beneficial assistance that I received during KEY pivotal times in my life that helped me grow into the person I am today by the grace of God.

I thank God that I have found rest and am finally secure, wealthy, happy, balanced, prosperous, and fulfilled. Through the Centre for Personal Excellence, I have chosen to contribute to others from my academic knowledge, spiritual understanding, and practical life experiences. I regularly conduct coaching sessions, seminars, training courses, and motivational speaking events, addressing topics from "Keys to SUCCESS" and "LIVING Your Ideal Life" to kingdom principles and connecting to spiritual wisdom. I am now truly living an ABUNDANT LIFE, in the will of God!

FOUR—MARRIAGE RESTORATION BY M. L.

About three months ago I found out my husband was cheating on me, and I kicked him out. I really didn't know what to do, and then his friend bought me the *How God Can and Will Restore Your Marriage* book. I read it and it changed me so much. Then I saw that God had to change the things in me He wanted, before He brought my husband home.

Only one month later, my husband came to spend the weekend with the kids. At the end of the weekend, he could see such a difference that he asked to come home. He was home for two months and then he went with the same friend, who gave me the book, to a flea market of all places. There my husband met a man who witnessed to him, and he got saved right there in the middle of the flea market crowd. Praise be to our God.

Our marriage and our life have been great ever since! God hears your prayers and has His perfect timing for everything—just obey and let God take over.

FIVE—HEALING AND RESTORATION OF MARRIAGE

For 23 years my husband was an alcoholic. This caused many problems in our marriage. Over the years, my husband was admitted to various rehabilitation centers, but every time it seemed like the problem worsened when he left the center. I could not understand why such a good man would waste his life in this way.

In December 2001, I moved out of the house and went to live 25 km out of town. Our son, who was in matriculation at the time, and our daughter stayed with their father. Early one morning at about five o'clock, I received a phone call from my daughter. She told me that my husband was in the hospital because he was vomiting blood.

I rushed to the hospital and found my husband in a bad shape as he had lost a large amount of blood. According to the doctors, his life hung by a thread and he could have died if our children had found him a half hour later.

I sat next to his bed and asked him if he didn't want to make King Jesus head of his life. He could help him with his drinking problem. My husband decided to do it.

God not only healed him from his alcohol addiction, but He also saved and restored our marriage completely. On March 6 this year, my husband will be free from alcohol for ten years. All glory goes to God for this huge miracle."[12]

SIX—IT HAPPENED FOR A REASON—GOD HAD A PLAN![13]

My husband had moved out and was living with a coworker. He was not happy and felt unwanted in twenty plus years of marriage. Prior to deciding to fight for our marriage, I had sent him emails quoting Scripture and pointing out his sins and faults. That was the wrong way to handle things! He has since shared with me that it just made him mad and confirmed for him that he had done the right thing by leaving.

---

12 Restore Ministry website.

13 Lydia, Restore Ministry website.

After approximately six weeks of separation and moving toward divorce, I realized that divorce did not have to be the answer. I decided to "fight the good fight." I was doing it alone with my prayers. A pastor friend across the country referred me to the Restore Ministries website. I immediately ordered the *Restore Your Marriage* book and read it within a couple of days.

I knew that God would restore our marriage; it was only a matter of days before I began to see changes in myself and would stop to think about what I had done to change. I realized it was not me—it was God working in awesome ways! The changes came after I began to realize the things I had done wrong, prayed for God to change me, and prayed for our marriage. I had to turn it all over to God and trust Him completely.

My husband couldn't imagine that the changes were real and that I wasn't putting on a front, trying to get him back for the wrong reasons. We did not talk much but would occasionally email to discuss the kids. Just as it was mentioned in the book, he tested me at times when he talked to me. I felt this happen on several occasions where he would say something to see if I would react. I did not react as I would have in the past, which showed him that I was a new person.

It was December 28th when my husband showed up at the resort where I was. I did not expect it, and my husband didn't know until 30 minutes prior to leaving our hometown for the resort that he would return home. He wasn't sure why he was there, but I assured him it was God who had brought him.

Ladies, be sure to turn it all over to God. I found that so many things happened just as the book said they would in the RYM book. I followed her advice, read the Scriptures, and prayed, and that is what got me through. It will get you through also.

"If God brings you to it, He will bring you through it." All of this happened for a reason. God had a plan, and now my husband and I are so much happier. We are living for God, we have a great marriage, and it just gets better every day! Thank you, Erin, for your ministry. It is so awesome how you have helped so many marriages, ours included! God is wonderful, and what a gift He has given the two of you!

SEVEN—GOD MOVED SO QUICKLY[14]

There aren't words enough to praise God for who He is and what He alone can do! He is the God of the impossible! His love for us is deeper and wider and higher than we could ever imagine. He loves blessing us and asks so little in return. Obedience with faith and repentance bring healing.

This is my second marriage. I had been married once before (when I was not a believer) and left that marriage in hatred and anger. This time was completely different, because of God's grace!

When my husband was gone, the Lord continually encouraged me and showed me through Scripture and through others that our marriage would be restored. He reminded me that it would be He who would soften my husband's heart as I sought and obeyed.

I found out about RMI when I was at church talking to a divorced woman; she gave me your pamphlet and shared her situation with me. I came home, immediately researched your website, and ordered the materials the very next day. I ordered the first resource packet and right away I read the book on restoring your marriage, which is excellent.

---

14 By Shelia.

Although the Lord had impressed upon me that our marriage would be restored, my husband had filed for divorce, so I ordered the book *Facing Divorce* as well. I responded without a lawyer, and—praise the Lord!—it was your book that the Lord used to convict me of all my sins. I already had a close walk with the Lord, but I needed to put God first in all things. God spoke daily to my heart and gave me the strength and faith to obey. I have watched a miracle unfold, and I give Him all the glory!

My neighbors, who were missionaries for 20 years, have a restored marriage after the wife read your book in just one day!

I have already shared your website with at least ten women and want to tell the world about it! I am recommending your resources to friends in both difficult and good marriages—I think every woman should do the workbook no matter the state of her marriage! I am buying a copy for our son and daughter-in-law, as well as for our daughter who is falling in love. I wish every woman could have your workbook before she gets married!

He is the Healer and Restorer, Redeemer and Lover of our souls. I praise Him day and night, always and forever.

My divorce was to be final; but my husband had it dismissed ONE day before. God works in just the right time even when I thought it was hopeless and wanted to give up. I kept going back again and again to all of Erin's books, and praying.

I finally gave up and trusted God to do what I could not do for myself. My husband moved back home and we are sharing what we have learned with others. I have had the opportunity to start a small group fellowship in my church and have given books to anyone who has shared with me that they, too, are going through separation or divorce.

Through the hard work and determination of Erin, this experience has truly changed my life! It has restored and changed my marriage into what God intended for us to have, not another statistic of divorce.

I have only love and utter gratefulness that this site and fellowship was there for me when there was no other solution to what I believed to be a hopeless situation. I am reminded every day of the promise He has kept that shows the LOVE my God has for me.

ALL THINGS ARE POSSIBLE THROUGH CHRIST, which means your marriage too. God bless you and thank you.

PRAYER

Almighty God, we confess we are a little slow on the maintenance sometimes. We start to believe the lies of the evil one, which say that we cannot be repaired, restored, and renewed. Your Word claims otherwise. Strengthen Your Word in us, Lord. That we might deepen in relationship with you for Your glory. Amen.

"Come," the Greatest Lover is Calling You

God loves each and every one of us so much. He loves us beyond comprehension. John 3:16-17 in the Amplified Bible declares,

> "For God so greatly loved and dearly prized the world that He [even] gave up His only begotten (unique) Son, so that whoever believes in (trusts in, clings to, relies on) Him shall not perish (come to destruction, be lost) but have eternal (everlasting) life. For God did not send the Son into the world in order to judge (to reject, to condemn, to pass sentence on) the world, but that the world might find salvation and be made safe and sound through Him."

He offers us the most beautiful gift. It is the gift of salvation. He offers us the gift of salvation through Jesus Christ, His only begotten Son. He is calling you to come and take freely the water of life.

> "The [Holy] Spirit and the bride (the church, the true Christians) say, Come! And let him who is listening say, Come! And let everyone come who is thirsty [who is painfully conscious of his need of those things by which

the soul is refreshed, supported, and strengthened]; and whoever [earnestly] desires to do it, let him come, take, appropriate, and drink the water of Life without cost"

(Revelation 22:17, AMP)

WHY DOES HUMANKIND NEED SALVATION?

Romans 6:23 tells us that, "The wages which sin pays is death, but the [bountiful] free gift of God is eternal life through (in union with) Jesus Christ our Lord" (AMP). We have all broken God's commandments and, for that reason, humankind is lost spiritually. The Bible says that the "wages of sin is death."

What is a wage? Every worker deserves a wage or salary. It is what we earn for our efforts, be it good or bad. We have all sinned and therefore we all have earned death. The Bible says in Ezekiel 18:20, "The soul that sins, it [is the one that] shall die. The son shall not bear and be punished for the iniquity of the father, neither shall the father bear and be punished for the iniquity of the son; the righteousness of the righteous shall be upon him only, and the wickedness of the wicked shall be upon the wicked only" (AMP).

Since humankind has broken God's commandments, sin has separated us from God. The Lord God is holy and cannot permit sin in His presence. The Bible tells us that even if a person breaks just one commandment, it is like breaking them all. James 2:10 tells us: "For whosoever keeps the Law [as a] whole but stumbles and offends in one [single instance] has become guilty of [breaking] all of it" (AMP). This means that even if we break one commandment, it is as if we broke them all for we stand guilty before a holy God. That is God's holy standard.

None of us have kept every commandment. We have broken God's Law. We are all sinners. God's justice requires that sin receive its full penalty. However, the suffering and sacrificial death of the Lord Jesus upon the cross satisfied the requirements of God's justice. Jesus Christ died for our sins. He suffered the penalty of the Law we had broken. Jesus suffered our punishment—He took our place because of his love for us. And we have seen and do testify that the Father sent the Son to be the Savior of the world (1 John 4:14).

God loves us and He desires to have a close relationship with us, but sin separates us from God. The Bible tells us that *all* on this earth have sinned and have fallen short of God's glory (Romans 3:23). When Adam and Eve first sinned in the Garden of Eden, they brought sin upon all humankind and the close fellowship that they had with God was no longer possible because of their sin. They suffered spiritual death and lost their special relationship with the Father.

The Lord instructed His people to make unblemished animal sacrifices for their sin. The Bible tells us that "Without shedding of blood there is no remission" for sin (Hebrews 9:22 NKJV). The blood of these animals covered their sins, but the blood of animals could not actually take sins away. God had a wonderful plan to restore humankind unto Himself. This plan would take away the sins of the world. God sent His only begotten Son to become a man and to shed His blood and to die for our sins. The Lord Jesus never sinned and therefore willingly died for us— being the perfect and holy sacrifice for our sins. Our sins were laid upon Him as He died for us.

It was prophesied in the Old Testament, hundreds of years before Christ Jesus came, that Messiah would die a terrible death and would save His people from their sins and be raised from the dead. In the book of Isaiah, we read that Messiah would die for our iniquities: "But He was wounded for our transgressions, He was bruised for our guilt and iniquities; the chastisement [needful to obtain] peace and well-being for us was upon Him, and with the stripes [that wounded] Him we are healed and made whole. All we like sheep have gone astray, we have turned everyone to his own way; and the Lord has made to light upon Him the guilt and iniquity of us all" (Isaiah 53:5-6 AMP).

It is the Lord's intention that humankind is not condemned but saved through believing in His Son, but those who refuse to believe in Him are condemned already, because they do not believe in the name of the only begotten Son of God. There is no other way to heaven except through the Lord Jesus Christ. We all have sinned but He, being sinless, paid the price for our sins. The Lord Jesus was the sinner's substitute on the cross. Because He died for sinners, those who receive Him as their Savior are not indebted to pay the penalty for their sin. The wage of sin is death—but He died for our sin—and paid our penalty. The gift of God is eternal life through Jesus Christ our Lord.

Christ Jesus paid it all! He has made the way for fellowship back to God. In order to be saved, one must have complete faith in the Savior. Faith in the Lord Jesus is most necessary for we are justified by faith: "Therefore, since we are justified (acquitted, declared righteous, and given a right standing with God) through faith, let us [grasp the fact that we] have [the peace of reconciliation to hold and to enjoy] peace with God through our Lord Jesus Christ (the Messiah, the Anointed One)" (Romans 5:1 AMP).

The Lord Jesus said in John 3:3: "I assure you, most solemnly I tell you, that unless a person is born again (anew, from above), he cannot ever see (know, be acquainted with, and experience) the kingdom of God" (AMP). Because we are all descendants of Adam and are sinners, we must be born again of God's Spirit (a spiritual birth) in order to be saved. And this new birth is only possible through receiving the Lord Jesus Christ as our Savior and Redeemer.

God granted us a free will, and because of this He will not force Himself on anyone. But God wants His creation to come to Him and be saved. God's plan of salvation is so wonderful, but it is only wonderful to those who receive the Lord Jesus Christ as their Savior. Those who do not believe in Him will not have everlasting life. He told us in John 3:36, "And he who believes in (has faith in, clings to, relies on) the Son has (now possesses) eternal life. But whoever disobeys (is unbelieving toward, refuses to trust in, disregards, is not subject to) the Son will never see (experience) life, but [instead] the wrath of God abides on him. [God's displeasure remains on him; His indignation hangs over him continually" (AMP).

Jesus never sinned; His sacrifice of His own life paid the price for our sins. That is why He is called the Lamb of God—He is completely spotless and innocent. A New Testament prophet, John the Baptist, "saw Jesus coming to him and said, 'Look, the Lamb of God, who takes away the sin of the world!'" (John 1:29).

Christ Jesus died in preparation for Passover. He took upon Himself all the sins of the world and He shed His own blood that we might be saved. He died willingly for us: "No one has greater love [no one has shown stronger affection] than to lay down (give up) his own life for his friends" (John 15:13 AMP).

John 10:17-18 states, "For this [reason] the Father loves Me, because I lay down My [own] life—to take it back again. No one takes it away from Me. On the contrary, I lay it down voluntarily.

[I put it from Myself.] I am authorized and have power to lay it down (to resign it) and I am authorized and have power to take it back again. These are the instructions (orders) which I have received [as My charge] from My Father" (AMP).

Christ Jesus rose from the dead three days after His crucifixion, conquering death. All those who receive Him will live forever with Him and death shall have no power over them. Because of His resurrection, Christians can walk a victorious life through the power of the Holy Spirit. The true meaning of life begins upon this earth when one receives Christ because all sins are forgiven and the fellowship that Adam and Eve had with God in the Garden of Eden is restored once again in the life of the believer. And when Christians physically die, they go to live with Christ Jesus forever. God the Father sent His only begotten Son, the Lord Jesus, into the world to save the world because He loves us so much.

The Lord Jesus said in John 11:25-26, "I am [Myself] the Resurrection and the Life. Whoever believes in (adheres to, trusts in, and relies on) me, although he may die, yet he shall live; and whoever continues to live and believes in (has faith in, cleaves to, and relies on) me shall never [actually] die at all. Do you believe this?" (AMP).

Salvation is a free gift. This means that you cannot earn your way into heaven. Your good works will not get you to heaven. Being a good person cannot get you into heaven. You can never be good enough to get into heaven because even one sin will keep you out of heaven. Jesus has already paid the price for your sins. To say that you can save yourself is an insult to Him who gave His life for you. The Bible says that "all our righteous acts are like filthy rags" (Isaiah 64:6) and there is no way we can make it into heaven by our own works. The Bible says that we are saved by grace through faith and not of our own works (Ephesians 2:8-9). Salvation is a gift from God.

> For it is by free grace (God's unmerited favor) that you are saved (delivered from judgment and made partakers of Christ's salvation) through [your] faith. And this [salvation] is not of yourselves [of your own doing, it came not through your own striving], but it is the gift of God; Not because of works [not the fulfilment of the Law's demands], lest any man should boast. [It is not the result of what anyone can possibly do, so no one can pride himself in it or take glory to himself.
>
> (Ephesians 2:8-9, AMP)

You can accept God's wonderful free gift of salvation through Jesus Christ—or you can reject His gift. The choice is yours. God created you with a free will to choose. God will not force Himself on anyone. Those who receive Jesus receive the gift of eternal life and their sins are forgiven. Those who reject Him will die physically and spiritually, lost in their sins, and will have to face the wrath of God on the day of judgment.

Every person will face the Lord Jesus Christ someday. He will either be your Savior or He will be your Judge. Romans 1:18 states, "But God shows his anger from heaven against all sinful, wicked people who suppress the truth by their wickedness" (NLT).

Unbelief in Him is a grievous sin against the Savior and will be punished as such. As we read before, the Lord Jesus said, "He that believeth not is condemned already." The Bible says that those who die in their sins, apart from the Lord Jesus Christ, will go to the lake of fire eternally. Revelation 20:15 states, "And anyone whose name was not found recorded in the book of life was thrown into the lake of fire." But one does not have to go there.

BELIEVE ON THE LORD JESUS CHRIST, THE SAVIOR AND THE REDEEMER

The Bible says, "Believe on the Lord Jesus Christ and you shall be saved."

What does it mean to believe? Believe what the Bible says.

Believe that Jesus is God—the second person of the Trinity.

Believe that He became flesh and was born of a virgin.

Believe that He lived a pure and sinless life.

Believe that God the Father loves you and He sent His only begotten Son to die for your sins so you won't have to go to hell but instead have eternal life. Believe that the wrath of God abides in the sinner but that eternal life is provided through Jesus Christ. Believe that you cannot save yourself by your own good works.

> In this the love of God was made manifest (displayed) where we are concerned: in that God sent His Son, the only begotten or unique [Son], into the world so that we might live through Him. In this is love: not that we loved God, but that He loved us and sent His Son to be the propitiation (the atoning sacrifice) for our sins.
>
> (1 John 4:9-10, AMP)

Believe that Jesus Christ rose from the dead and that He is seated at the right hand of God the Father. Romans 8:34 asks, "Who is there to condemn [us]? Will Christ Jesus (the Messiah), who died, or rather who was raised from the dead, who is at the right hand of God actually pleading as He intercedes for us?" (AMP). Believe the words that Jesus said in the Bible. He said in John 14:6, "I am the Way and the Truth and the Life; no one comes to the Father except by (through) Me" (AMP).

> If you acknowledge and confess with your lips that Jesus is Lord and in your heart believe (adhere to, trust in, and rely on the truth) that God raised Him from the dead, you will be saved. For with the heart a person believes (adheres to, trusts in, and relies on Christ) and so is justified (declared righteous, acceptable to God), and with the mouth he confesses (declares openly and speaks out freely his faith) and confirms [his] salvation. The Scripture says, "No man who believes in Him [who adheres to, relies on, and trusts in Him] will [ever] be put to shame or be disappointed.   (Romans 10:9-11, AMP)

God says in Jeremiah 29:13: "And ye shall seek me, and find me, when ye shall search for me with all your heart" (KJV). We must seek God to live eternally.

If you have received Jesus Christ as your Lord and Savior, but the evidence of being born again is missing, please remember that we cannot generate change by trying harder. Self-effort never produces eternal life. Rather, we must return to the cross and consider the darkness of our sin and the brilliance of His love. "We love because He first loved us" (1 John 4:9). For only at the cross do we find forgiveness and the power to be transformed. Let's truly receive the forgiveness offered through faith in Jesus and then continue to grow with a victorious assurance that we are born again. Let's trust the truth of His Word, which has been given into our hands so we may know.

Salvation includes deliverance from the power of sin. Naturally we are all fond of evil, and we run after it greedily; we love the bond slaves of iniquity, and we loved the bondage.

This last is the worst feature of the case. But salvation delivers us from the power of sin. We learn sin is evil, and regard it as such, loathe it, repent of having ever been in love with it, and turns our back upon it. Then, through God's Spirit, the master of our lusts, we put the flesh beneath our feet, and rise into liberty as children of God.

Salvation includes deliverance from the present wrath of God, which abides upon unsaved people every moment of their life. Every person who is unforgiven is the object of divine wrath. "God is angry with the wicked every day. If he turn not, he will whet his sword" (Psalm 7:11-12). The probation period has ended. Sinners have been proved, and found to be unworthy; they have been "weighed in the balances, and found wanting" (Daniel 5:27 NJKV).

Every soul that is unreconciled to God by the blood of his Son is in the gall of bitterness. Salvation at once sets us free from this state of danger and alienation. We are no longer the "children of wrath, even as others" (Ephesians 2:3 KJV), but are made children of God and joint heirs with Christ Jesus. What can be c more precious than this?

I urge each person to see to this matter of their own salvation. Do it, I pray you, and in earnest, for no one can do it for you. I have asked God for your soul, and I pray I may have an answer of peace concerning you. But unless you also pray, my prayers are in vain.

THE GREAT INVITATION

"The [Holy] Spirit and the bride (the church, the true Christians) say, Come! And let him who is listening say,

Come! And let everyone come who is thirsty [who is painfully conscious of his need of those things by which the soul is refreshed, supported, and strengthened]; and whoever [earnestly] desires to do it, let him come, take, appropriate, and drink the water of Life without cost."

(Revelation 22:17, AMP)

The time is coming, and for some has come, when the Father, in love, will extend the last invitation for the lost to "come" and be saved by His grace. Before John closed the last book of the Bible (the Revelation of Jesus Christ), it is as though God said, "John, give the invitation one more time for the lost to come and be saved." Likewise, I am giving you the opportunity to come to Jesus and be saved.

The Holy Spirit, who indwells the bride (the Church), is inviting the lost, the downtrodden, the sick, the lame, the sinners, those who have previously known Him and are now backslidden, those who attended church but were never told that Christianity is an intimate relationship with Christ, those who want to have a "real" experience of Christ's love. Those in bondage of all kinds, those held down by strongholds, and those who need a new beginning—a new life, an open heaven. Those in physical and spiritual prison who are seeking total freedom. The word of God to you is "come today—do not delay!"

The Holy Spirit, who indwells the bride (Church), is inviting the lost to come and receive Christ and be saved, or simply come and receive Him anew. Let all those who are saved at this time of the last invitation join the Spirit and the bride by inviting others to "come" and be saved.

Jesus gave the same invitation 2000 years ago. He said, "If anyone thirsts, let him come to me and drink (John 7:37). At Jacob's well, Jesus said to the Samaritan woman, "Whoever drinks of this water that I shall give him will never thirst. But the water that I shall give him will become in him a fountain of water springing up into everlasting life" (John 4:13-14). God's promise to you is that you "will never thirst." In other words, salvation through Jesus Christ satisfies forever. "Whoever desires, let him take the water of life freely" (Revelation 22:17).

The apostle Peter tells us that we are "not redeemed [bought back from Satan and sin] with corruptible things, like silver or gold, ... but with the precious blood of Christ, as of a lamb without blemish and without spot" (1 Peter 1:18-19 NKJV).

This blood cleanses you from all sin—not some, but all; past, present, and future (1 John 1:7). However, it is not a license to go out and continue in sin. Without the shed blood of Jesus, there is no remission (forgiveness) of sin (Hebrews 9:22). Jesus loves us and washed us from all our sins in His own blood (Revelation 1:5).

If you have been reading this book and have seen the various references to the Great Invitation, the Salvation Prayer Template, and how to turn your life around and begin a wonderful relationship with Jesus, *now is the time—just come as you are.*

Jesus has made provision for your sin. *Everyone* is covered by His finished work on the cross. He who gives this warning and affirms and testifies to these things says, "Yes (it is true). [Surely] I am coming quickly (swiftly, speedily). Amen (so let it be)! Yes, come, Lord Jesus!" (Revelation 22:20 AMP).

A SALVATION PRAYER—COME TO HIM

If you do not know Jesus or have not confessed Him as your personal Savior or have backslidden into the world, now is the day of salvation. Do not let the enemy of your soul put fear inside you. Jesus says, "All that the Father gives me will come to me, and whoever comes to me I will never drive away" (John 6:37).

SALVATION PRAYER TEMPLATE

If you would like to begin a personal relationship with the greatest Lover and Savior of your soul, Jesus Christ, you can pray the following prayer today.

> *Heavenly Father, I come to You in the name of Jesus. I know You died on the cross for my sins and I want You to be the Lord of my life, now and forever in heaven. I am sorry for the many ways I have sinned against You, including abusing Your love for me and my selfish way of living. Please forgive me.*

> *Please, Lord, come into my life now as my Savior. Wash me clean, fill me with Your Spirit, and with Your help, I will learn to love and obey You as the Lord of my life. I confess with my mouth, "Jesus is Lord," and turn away from a life of sin. I believe in my heart that You raised Him from the dead.*

> *Thank You for forgiving me and bringing me back to You, God. Thank You for coming into my heart, for giving me Your Holy Spirit as You have promised, and for being Lord of my life. In Jesus' name, Amen!*

If you have prayed this prayer, you have been "born again." That is, you have been made a new creature in Christ. Your past does not belong to you anymore. Your life has begun anew. When Satan comes around trying to remind you of all your past deeds, just tell him, "Wrong door, you cannot come in. Sin no longer lives here!"

Having confessed Jesus as your Lord and Savior, you need to tell someone to witness to the fact that you now want to walk with God. Then find a Bible-believing church where you can have fellowship with believers. Make sure you also regularly read the Word of God as this gives truth and direction (Psalm 119:105). Irrespective of whatever circumstances life throws your way, He has promised that no one can take His children out of His hand (John 10:28). His presence surrounds you; the bond between you and the Lord cannot be broken. His banner over you is love (Song of Solomon 2:4).

NOTE: If you have received Jesus as your Lord and Savior using the above call to salvation, we would love to rejoice with you. Please share your story with us by sending an email to johnashomade@gmail.com. We promise to continue praying for you so that you may enter fully into Jesus' finished work on the cross.

Appendix of Love

PERSONAL NOTES FOR
YOUR REFLECTION/PRAYERS

This section has been created for you to encourage personal reflections after reading *Father Teach Me How to Love Again*, and also to help you pray for the manifestation of God's love already inside you.

> And hope maketh not ashamed; because the love of God
> is shed abroad in our hearts by the Holy Ghost which is
> given unto us.   (Romans 5:5)

Don't ever worry about not having enough love inside you. The Word says God's love is shed abroad in your heart by the Holy Ghost. God's love is already *in* you. All you need to do is let it flow *through* you.

PRAYER

Thank You for Your Word, Lord, and for Your ultimate gift of love when You died upon the cross for my sin and the sin of the world. In the days ahead, cause me to increase and excel and overflow with Your love and to be what this world needs most of all ... a living example of love. Amen.

Notes

Acknowledgements

My gratitude to Pastor Matthew Ashimolowo, the Senior Pastor and General Overseer of Kingsway International Christian Centre (KICC), I thank you for your strategic guidance, positive challenges to excel, and anointed teaching. It is a blessing to feed under an anointed teacher such as yourself.

To Apostle Ebenezer Olushola, the General Overseer and Founding Father of the Church of God's Grace worldwide. You are a real father with a heart for God and His children. I thank you for your love and prayers. The peculiar anointing you carry upon your life is now flowing from the shepherd to your sons in Christ, bringing healing to lives and deliverance to people.

To my special friend and pastor, Apostle Thomas Ojo, the General Overseer of Christ Temple International, you epitomize the love of Christ, and are always there for us irrespective of the circumstances.

To my pastor and friend, Pastor Sunny Inegbedoh of Global Harvester International, I thank you for taking a risk with me in facilitating my entering into my calling.

To all my friends, family members, and kingdom ministers who have spent copious time standing in the gap for me, I love and appreciate you beyond your imagination—blessings by the bushel. Thank you all.

About the Author

John Akeem Shomade is born in Nigeria to a Muslim family. He became a Christian after an encounter with the person of our Lord Jesus Christ. His code of conduct is integrity and love. Today, John is a pastor, teacher of the biblical principles and has an extensive itinerant ministry. He's also a trained chaplain and founder of the Agapeo Love International Ministries (A.L.I.M.) in the UK. He is married with two children.

John has found the secret of spiritual power—walking in love. This is what gives us power over most of the ills of today as we obey the greatest commandment given by Jesus, our Lord and Saviour. One of his desires is to call people to repentance and be reconciled with God through the saving power of Jesus' blood. He encourages people to start a personal relationship with our Heavenly Father.